COMPUTER WORLD

By Jacquetta Megarry

A Piccolo Factbook

Contents

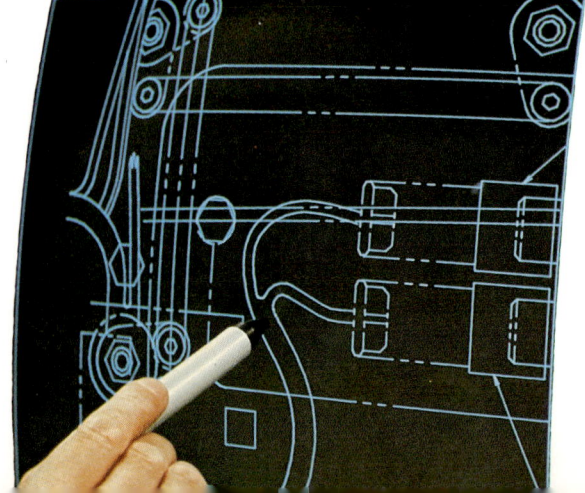

COMPUTER WORLD

By Jacquetta Megarry

Adviser: Dr. Michael Thorne
Editor: Jacqui Bailey
Designer: David Jefferis

A Piccolo Factbook

Can Machines Think?

Computers are changing the world. In many countries today industry, banks, and airlines rely on them. Computers are used in schools and homes. Science, technology and space research all depend on them.

Unfortunately, many people think of computers as being mysterious and even threatening; and the unfamiliar words computer people use all the time do not help. This book looks at the computer simply as a powerful tool – a good servant but a bad master. Unfamiliar words are introduced in **bold** and explained in the Glossary (pages 88-91).

The computer revolution

In the past, certain inventions have caused great changes in our way of life. The printing press led to an age of books, libraries and later to newspapers. Steam power and electricity made life less physically demanding by increasing human muscle-power. But we are still adjusting to the effects of the industrial revolution which they created. Today, computers are capable of many jobs which we once thought could only be done by human brains. If these machines can increase our 'brain-power', the effects will be far-reaching indeed. But can a machine be 'intelligent'?

What is intelligence?

Intelligence can mean a number of different things. If you say that a person is intelligent, you might mean that he or she does well at maths or French, or talks in a clever way. Or, you could mean that they are good at fixing things that go wrong.

For all their remarkable powers, the computers of today are mostly not intelligent when judged on these sort of tasks. To begin with, they cannot do anything at all without being given instructions by humans. These are contained in a **program**, without which a computer is useless.

It is easy to program a computer to do calculations, which it works through unbelievably fast. With a lot more thought, it can also be programmed to solve problems, crack codes and play games like chess.

However, we are only just becoming successful at writing programs which allow computers to recognize human speech and handwriting. It is very hard to make a computer do some things we find easy, like recognizing solid objects from pictures. Every instruction has to be spelt out in great detail because computers have no way of 'filling in' anything that has been left out – unlike humans who are able to use their 'common sense'.

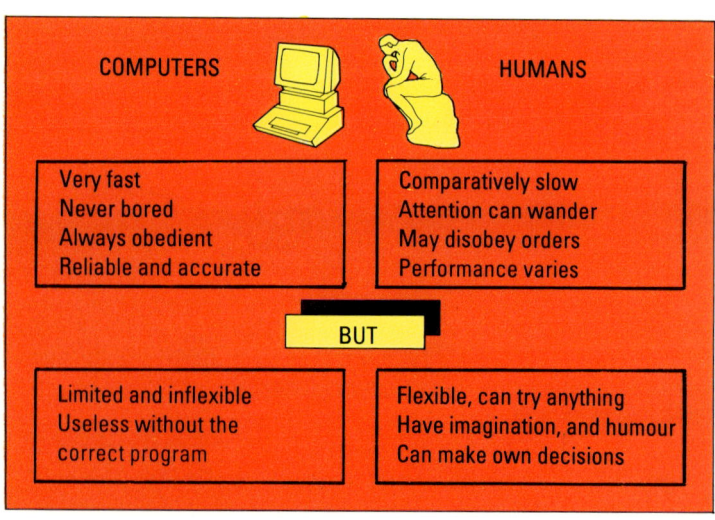

COMPUTERS   HUMANS

Very fast	Comparatively slow
Never bored	Attention can wander
Always obedient	May disobey orders
Reliable and accurate	Performance varies

BUT

Limited and inflexible	Flexible, can try anything
Useless without the correct program	Have imagination, and humour
	Can make own decisions

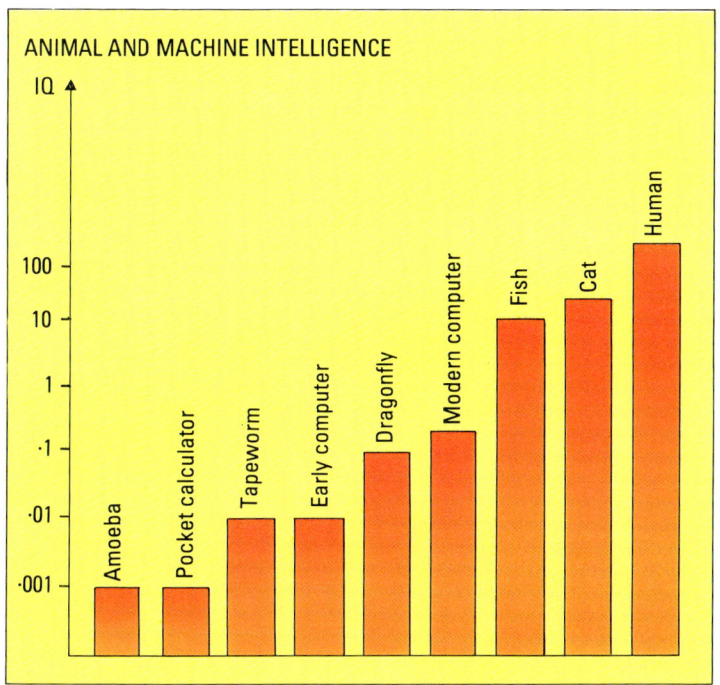

ANIMAL AND MACHINE INTELLIGENCE

IQ

100
10
1
·1
·01
·001

Amoeba
Pocket calculator
Tapeworm
Early computer
Dragonfly
Modern computer
Fish
Cat
Human

Animal versus computer

In the human and animal world, intelligence varies widely. The bar chart above shows, in a very rough way, how machine intelligence might be compared with that of different animals.

If the average human has an IQ of 100, an amoeba, which is *much* less intelligent, could be rated at ·001 points. A pocket calculator is only around amoeba level. Although the amoeba can't do sums, it can at least react to the world around it.

The first computers were much more 'intelligent' than pocket calculators, but could only do very limited tasks. Several experts have rated their IQs at tapeworm level (around ·01). Modern computers are very much faster, and their programs make them more adaptable. They are now about level with the dragonfly (IQ around ·1).

However, even a modern computer is not nearly as intelligent as a fish or a cat, which can understand and respond to changes.

Hardware and Software

Many people find the idea of an 'intelligent machine' disturbing. How can switches, wires and electric currents add up to intelligence?

To understand this idea, we first have to separate the computer's hardware from its software. **Hardware** is the general name given to all the equipment which makes up the computer – the boxes and the screens.

Hardware is all quite useless without the **software**. Software is the name for both the programs, which contain instructions, and the information or **data** that the computer has to work on.

Software is usually prepared in advance and stored on tape cassettes or **discs**. These are **loaded** into the computer when someone is ready to use it. This is like loading a hi-fi system with a pre-recorded disc or tape cassette of music (see below).

A 'one-track mind'

A hi-fi system can only do one thing – it reproduces sounds. Early computers

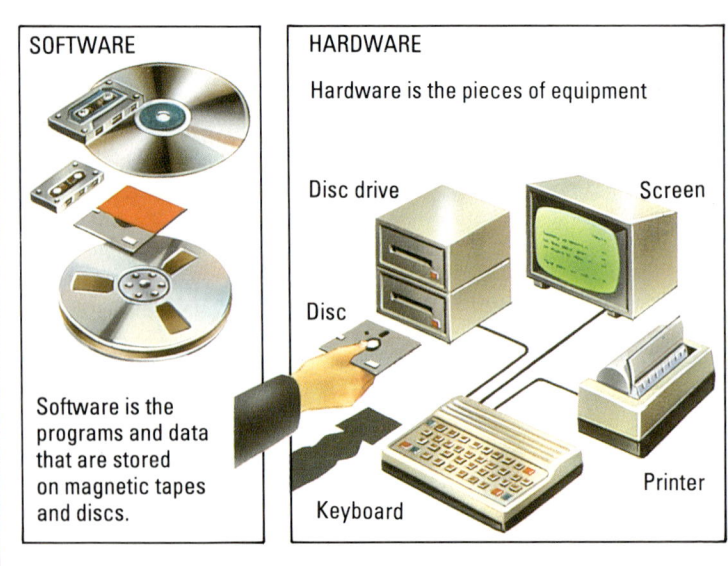

SOFTWARE

Software is the programs and data that are stored on magnetic tapes and discs.

HARDWARE

Hardware is the pieces of equipment

Disc drive

Screen

Disc

Keyboard

Printer

were a bit like this. They could only do one job because their programs were wired into them.

The secret of making a computer truly general-purpose was to separate the software from the hardware. That way, a code-breaking machine could be turned into a chess-playing machine just by loading a different program. It is like the difference between a music-box and a piano; one can only play the tune that is built into it, whereas the other can be made to play whatever music the pianist chooses to play.

Record

Turntable

In a hi-fi the music on the record is software, the turntable is hardware

In the forty years or so since general-purpose computers have been available, people have developed more and more advanced programs. These can make a computer do any job that can be spelt out in detail.

The main use of computers nowadays is data processing. 'Processing' data simply means that the computer works on it. The data (information) is usually in words or numbers. But, with suitable hardware and software, computers can also process pictures, music and speech.

Programmed to 'learn'

A lot of everyday computing only seems clever because huge amounts of data are processed very quickly. Often the processes themselves are fairly simple, like adding numbers. However, advanced programs can 'learn from experience', a bit like humans do.

Some computers have huge memories, and can search through them in seconds. A chess-playing program can 'improve its game' by making the computer store the results of the different strategies it plays, and then making it repeat the successful ones.

The Turing Test

The bar chart on page 9 shows a remarkable example of rapid evolution. Even though the computer's IQ may not look impressive when compared with that of a human, think how quickly it has increased.

It took us humans about two million years to reach our present level of intelligence. Yet in less than forty years, computers have already overtaken lower forms of life and are continuing to 'evolve' very quickly. Whilst new discoveries constantly increase computer power, it looks as if **artificial intelligence** will continue to increase also. Will it ever reach the point where we would say that a computer can actually *think*? How would we know if it did?

Human or computer?

The Turing Test for Thinking Machines was suggested by a brilliant mathematician called Alan Turing. He pointed out that we can only deduce that humans are able to think from what they say or write. We cannot judge a computer fairly because we can see it is 'just a machine'. So the Turing Test puts the judge in a separate room from the computer. A third room contains another human. The computer and

QUESTION

How many curves?

How many loose ends?

Is it C?

Is it J?

How many horizontals?

How many verticals?

Is it S?

ANSWER

One

Two

You haven't got enough
information yet to get the
right answer. How do you
know it isn't J, for example?

That's another guess. How do
you know it isn't C, for
example?

None.

None. Good question

Wrong. Your guess conflicts
with what you know already.
Remember that the letter has
one curve

the human are each linked
to **terminals** that are in the
same room as the judge so
that messages can be ex-
changed.

The judge's job is to work
out which messages come
from the human and which
from the computer. If the
judge cannot tell the difference, Turing argued, the
computer can be said to
think.

For example, look at the
'conversation' shown on the
two printers on the left. One
was connected to a compu-
ter, the other to a human.
Which do you think was
which? Can you be sure?
Could both have been
humans? If so, which was
showing more intelligence?

The Alphabet Game
The conversation shows an
alphabet guessing game.
One player chooses a letter,
and the other has to guess
what it is by asking questions about its shape. The
object of the game is to
identify the letter with as
few questions as possible.
The questioner is supposed
to work it out, though, not
just guess.

Before turning the page to
find out what the letter is,
you might like to work out
which letters would fit the
clues given here. For example, the answer of "Two" to
"How many loose ends?" still
leaves four possible letters.
Can you work them out?

13

QUESTION	ANSWER
How many curves?	One
How many loose ends?	Two
Is it C?	You haven't got enough information yet to get the right answer. How do you know it isn't J, for example?
Is it J?	That's another guess. How do you know it isn't C, for example?
How many horizontals?	None. Good, this rules out one possibility.
How many verticals?	None. Good question.
Is it S?	Wrong. Your guess conflicts with what you know already. Remember that the letter has *one* curve.
Is it C?	Yes. Well done. Do you want to play again?

Here is another look at the same conversation, with some notes alongside it. Notice that direct answers are not always given; sometimes questions are met with further questions, or comments like "That's another guess".

In fact, both sides of the conversation require some thought, as you will find out if you try playing the game with a friend. You must start by choosing a particular style of lettering, though, like the one shown at the top of these pages.

In this case it was a human who asked the questions. Answers and comments were given by the computer. You might think that these show more 'intelligence' than the questions.

However, this game does not prove that a computer can pass the Turing Test. A judge could easily have caught out the computer by asking a different question, like "Which is your favourite letter?"

The computer cannot 'think out' the answer for

OPQRSTUVWXYZ

NOTES

This rules out all the letters with no curves (AEFHIKLMNTVWXYZ) and also all those with two or more (BRS).

This rules out all the letters with no loose ends (DO) and those with one (PQ), C,G,J and U are all still possible.

Guesses are not encouraged! The next question ought to rule out one or two possibilities.

Another guess! What question should be asked?

This rules out the letter G.

This rules out both J and U in one go. (There's only one answer left which fits the facts.)

Forgetful!

The right answer.

each letter. It has to be 'taught' how to answer the questions for every letter in the alphabet before the game begins. The table below shows one way of doing this. The first five letters have been filled in; try finishing off the rest.

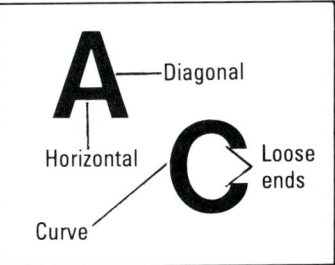

	0	1	2	3+
Verticals	AC	BDE		
Horizontals	BCD	A		E
Diagonals	BCDE		A	
Curves	AE	CD	B	
Loose ends	BD		AC	E

Notice that the computer was doing much more than just answering the questions about the shape of its chosen letter. It was making judgements about whether the questions were 'good' or 'bad'. This is a much more complicated task.

Of course, it is not the computer itself that makes these judgements, but its software. How do you make a program do this?

Planning the software

The first step in writing a computer program is to break the job down into manageable bits. Think of it as a problem that has to be done in stages. A **flow chart** is one way of showing the main stages of a problem and how they are related.

Once a flow chart has been worked out, writing a program can be fairly routine. It has to be written in a special language, though (see pages 74-75). And it is essential to get every little detail right as computers have no 'common sense'. They obey every instruction exactly, including any mistakes the programmer might make. That is why you hear stories about computers sending out bills for £0.00; someone forgot to tell it not to!

Right: This flow chart shows the main stages that are needed in a program for the Alphabet Game.

What a flow chart means

Flow charts show what decisions have to be made, what questions have to be answered to make those decisions, and how one question leads to another. If the solution to a problem can be written down in a flow chart, it can usually be programmed for a computer.

The program for the Alphabet Game first has to decide if a question is a general one like "How many curves?", or a specific one like "Is it C?". Look at the left branch of the flow chart opposite. If a question rules out no possibilities, it is wasted. If it rules out many possibilities, it is a good question.

The right side of the chart shows how the program will deal with specific guesses. These are first checked to see if they match up with the information already given. If the guess was made on too little evidence, other possible letters are suggested. Only if the right letter is found by asking the right questions does the program confirm the answer.

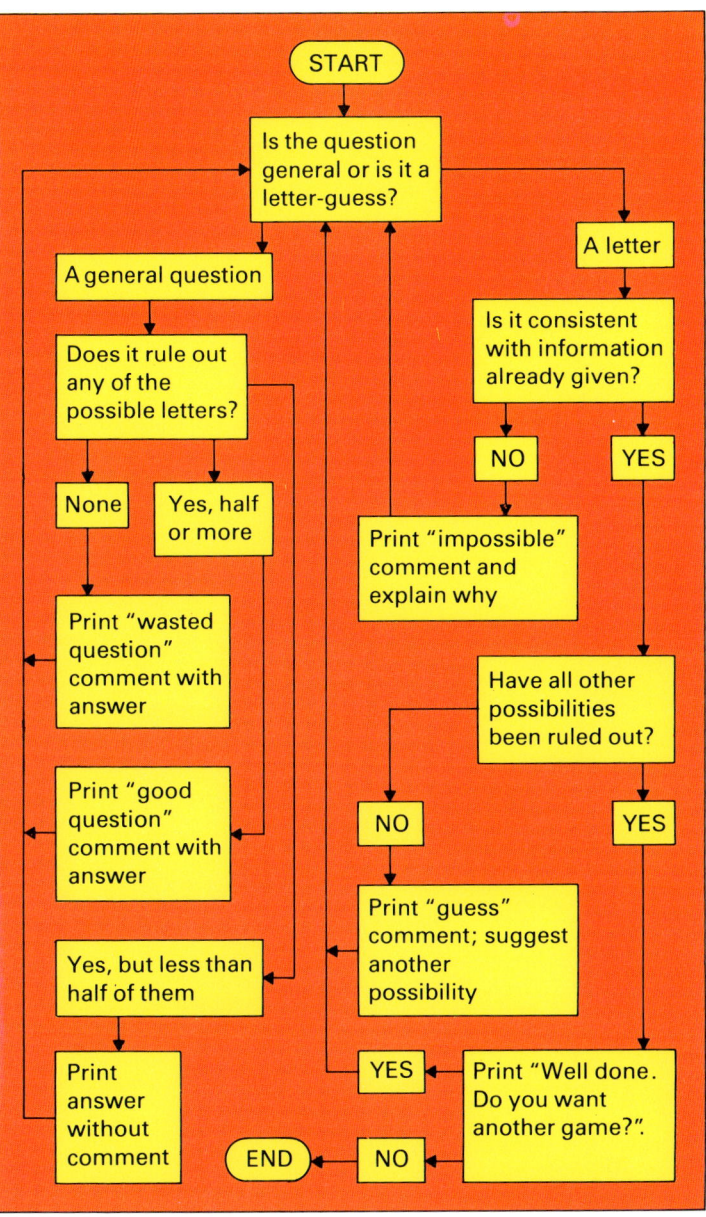

START

Is the question general or is it a letter-guess?

A general question

A letter

Does it rule out any of the possible letters?

Is it consistent with information already given?

None

Yes, half or more

NO

YES

Print "impossible" comment and explain why

Print "wasted question" comment with answer

Print "good question" comment with answer

Have all other possibilities been ruled out?

NO

YES

Yes, but less than half of them

Print "guess" comment; suggest another possibility

Print answer without comment

YES

Print "Well done. Do you want another game?".

END

NO

17

Enter the Microchip

It is over a century since Sir Charles Babbage invented the first computer, but his 'Analytical Engine' was never built. A computer needs thousands of parts, all linked up and made to work together; this could not be done with mechanical parts. The first working computers were built in the 1940s, using electronic parts.

Progress since then has been spectacular. A modern **microcomputer** is 10,000 times cheaper and vastly more reliable than its ancestors. It is much smaller – up to 50,000 times – but, almost incredibly, it works much faster and can handle much more information. If motor car technology had made similar progress, a Rolls Royce would now be as cheap as this book; more powerful than any train; could go round the world 2500 times on a tankful of petrol and would be so small that you could park six on this full stop.

1970s computer

1980s computer

Below: ENIAC, one of the first generation of mainframe computers. Above: A second generation computer. Right: A modern microcomputer.

In terms of size and speed, the first three generations of computers can be likened to a dinosaur, an elephant and a greyhound.

Size and speed

The 'first-generation' computers of the 1940s took years to build and cost a small fortune. They had thousands of parts, weighed many tonnes and used great lengths of cable. They filled huge rooms, which had to be air-conditioned to stop them overheating because of the amount of power they used.

They depended on thousands of valves, which were a bit like complicated and unreliable light bulbs. So the computer was always breaking down, and skilled engineers had to be always on the spot.

In 1948, the discovery of the **transistor** launched the 'second generation'. Just as transistors made radios much smaller, cheaper and more reliable, so it was with computers. Transistors were mostly made from silicon, which is cheaply obtained from ordinary sand. They do not overheat and can be packed much more closely than valves. Still, one transistor generally replaced one valve.

The real breakthrough came in the 1960s, with the famous silicon **chip**. Tiny chips, just a few millimetres across, can carry **integrated circuits**. A few of these can replace hundreds of transistors and metres of wire. This made the 'third generation' of computers incredibly powerful, cheap and compact compared with the first two. Now, there is a 'fourth generation' of computers, with a complete computer **processor** on a single chip.

Computers of the first generation became as extinct as the dinosaur within twenty years of being a major invention. The second generation made a major step forward, but the third and fourth generations have far outstripped the first two.

Below: From left to right: a valve, some transistors, a silicon chip (actual size).

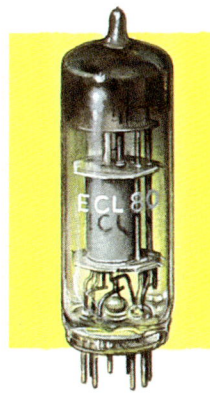 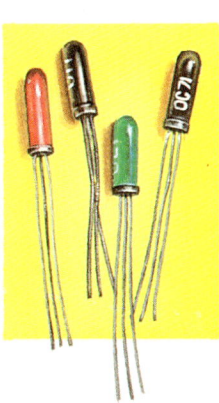 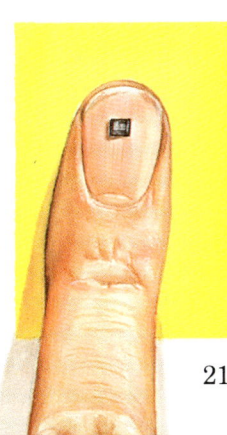

21

Chips with Everything

The silicon chip has had an enormous impact because of its amazing combination of power, speed, size, reliability and cheapness. Chips use verv little power – less than 1/1000th of a light bulb – so they can work inside battery-powered devices. Because the wiring is built into the chip, it is sturdy. Many chips can also work well even in extremely hot or cold temperatures.

Although making chips is complicated and must be carried out under carefully controlled conditions, the raw material is very cheap and huge numbers can be made in each batch. Therefore, as long as there is a high demand for a particular type of chip, it can be made very cheaply indeed.

The result has been that computing power has been added to a wide range of everyday machines. For example, gone are the days

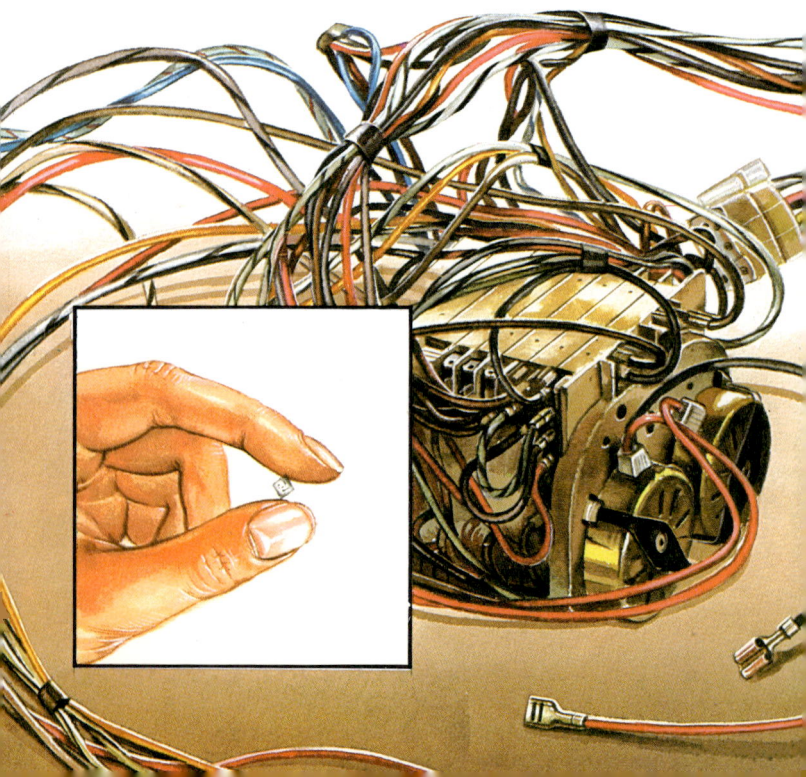

when watches were just expected to tell the time. They may now have built-in alarms, stopwatches, calculators, musical chimes, video games and miniature radios – all controlled by a silicon chip inside a normal-sized wristwatch.

Smaller and smaller

Size is important in modern computers. Electrical impulses travel at the speed of light (330,000 km/s). In early machines, fractions of a second would be wasted while messages travelled along metres of cable. But this hardly mattered, as the

Left: The device in a washing machine that controlled wash times and temperatures. Inset: the chip that has replaced it.

Above: The chip inside a disc camera controls the exposure time and advances the film, leaving the photographer free to think about the subject of the picture he wants to take.

computers themselves operated more slowly. Nowadays, computers work so incredibly quickly that their speed is measured in thousand millionths of a second. So it has become important to shorten the distances over which messages have to be sent inside the computer.

Each year, more and more parts are being packed onto every chip. In fact, the complexity of the tiny integrated circuits has just about *doubled* each year since they were invented!

Making a Chip

A modern computer uses silicon chips for its processor and for its **memory**. Some computers use a number of chips for different parts of the processor. The latest microcomputers have a complete processing unit on one chip, a **microprocessor**.

A tiny crystal is dipped into pure melted silicon. As it cools, it 'grows' to about one metre in length.

There are also different kinds of chip for different parts of the memory. To the naked eye, one chip looks much like another. However, the microscopic circuits sealed into each chip may be very different.

A lot of work is needed to design and test a circuit for a particular type of chip. So it is only worth doing if there is a big demand for chips of the same design. However, once a circuit has been designed, that chip can be made in large numbers quite cheaply. One wafer of silicon about 100mm in diameter will make hundreds of chips, although most of these will be rejected as faulty.

A diamond saw cuts the large crystal into thousands of thin round wafers, which are polished mirror-smooth.

Conditions have to be very carefully controlled. Furnaces must be kept at exactly the right temperature and mixture of gases. Equipment and people must be absolutely clean and free of dust.

Computers help to design and test the circuit for the chip. Then they separate the design into different layers.

4

Each layer is printed onto a photomask, which can carry hundreds of tiny images of the same design.

7

Each wafer is sliced into hundreds of chips. 70–90% were marked as faulty when tested; these are rejected.

5

Each photomask prints its pattern of images onto the wafer. The wafer is then sealed in a hot furnace.

8

The surviving chips are tested again, then wired up to metal contacts with gold wire, finer than human hair.

6

Every tiny circuit on the wafer is tested many times, using fine needles to touch the electrical contacts.

9

After more tests, the good chips are mounted on plastic with two rows of metal pins, ready to be used.

Inside the Computer

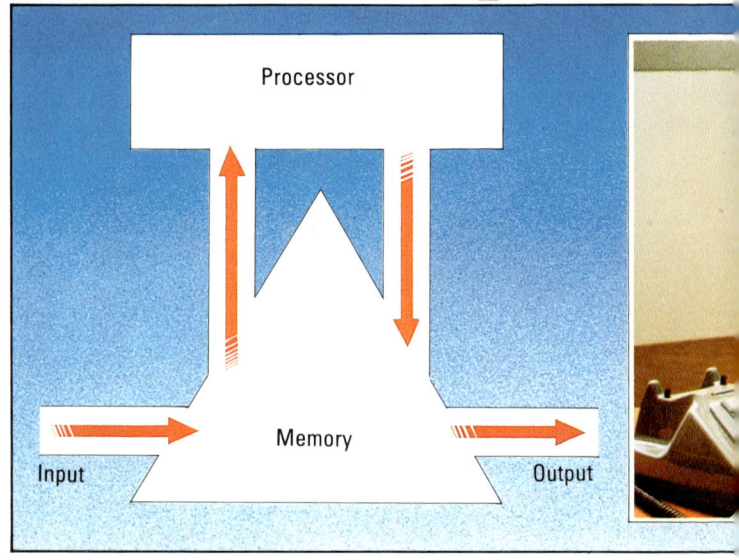

Both humans and computers deal with information in four basic stages, as shown in the diagram above. With humans, 'input' is any information about the outside world which we gather through our senses. For example, the man shown on the right is receiving input from the telephone and from the computer **screen**. It is then stored in his 'memory' and 'processed' by his brain. This results in 'output' in the form of speech or writing.

If the input is a sum like $\frac{1}{2}+\frac{1}{3}=?$, he has to remember facts about numbers, and rules about how to add fractions. After processing the problem, he can then output the answer.

A computer's **input** has to be specially prepared for it. Programs and data have to be put into exactly the right form and then fed in through an input device – often a keyboard connected to the computer.

Computers have only a limited amount of memory built into them, and some of it 'forgets' whenever the computer is switched off. So computers also have 'external memory' stores – tapes

or discs on which software can be recorded and held until it is needed. Even humans sometimes refer to 'external memory' – for example, to reference books.

The processor
The processor is the 'brain' of the computer. It receives programs and data from an input device and sends the answer to an **output** device. In the sum mentioned above, for example, a program for adding fractions would be sent to the processor with the data ($\frac{1}{2}$, $\frac{1}{3}$). It works out the answer ($\frac{5}{6}$) and sends it

Humans and computers both deal with information in four basic stages.

to the output device – usually a screen.

Almost all computers have output devices as separate pieces of equipment. Microcomputers have an input device (keyboard), processor and internal memory all packaged together. Large, or **mainframe**, computers have separate pieces of equipment for each stage. Examples of some different microcomputers are shown on pages 78 to 81.

Analogue and Digital

Deep down inside, a computer's operations are **digital**. Digital means that something has been broken down into units. However, many everyday things, like the movement of time and temperature, are **analogue** – they change continuously.

With an ordinary watch the hands move smoothly around the watch face. We estimate the time from the positions of the moving hands. On a digital watch, however, the time is shown in numbers. It is either exactly 12.43 and 23 seconds or 12.43 and 24 seconds. It can never be shown as in between.

Temperature, like time, varies smoothly. However, a digital thermometer shows the temperature as exact numbers.

Nearly all modern computers are digital. No matter

ANALOGUE

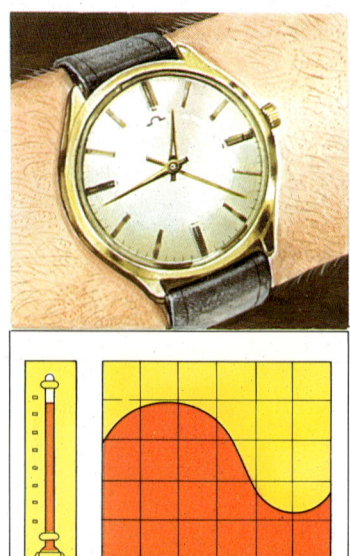

DIGITAL

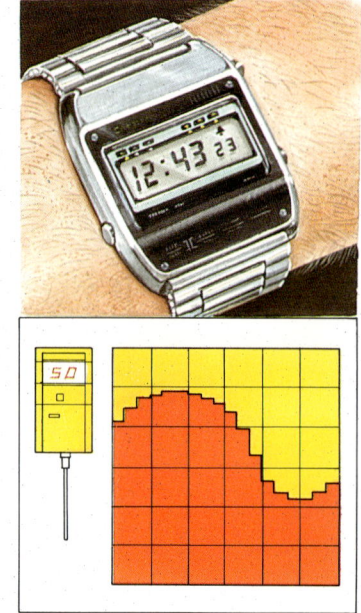

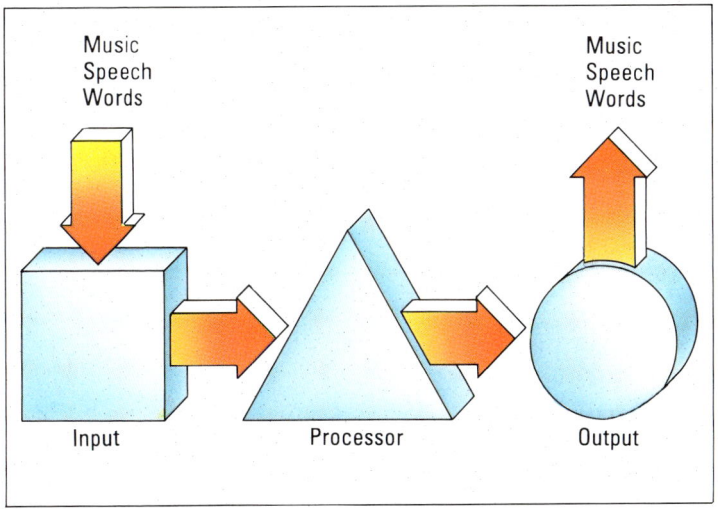

Music
Speech
Words

Music
Speech
Words

Input   Processor   Output

what form the input takes – letters, drawings or speech – it has to be turned into digits, or numbers, before the processor is able to deal with it.

The binary system

We are used to a counting system that is based on ten numbers, from 0 to 9. Computers use the **binary** system, which is based on just two numbers, 0 and 1. On page 76, you can see how a 'base-ten' number can be turned into its 'base-two' equivalent.

Humans find base-ten numbers more manageable than long strings of 1s and 0s. However, it is easier to design computers to work on

The processor works in binary. Input devices code information into binary form, and output devices decode it again.

the binary system. This is because a computer turns information into electric currents. Inside the processor, thousands of tiny electrical switches turn the currents either 'on' or 'off', to represent '1' or '0'.

Input devices have to translate everything that is fed into the computer into a code made of these binary numbers. Output devices then turn the processor's binary output back into a form which humans can more easily understand.

Input Devices

Input devices feed information into the computer. In the early days, input was usually prepared on a separate machine which punched holes in cards or paper tape. A hole meant a 1, and no hole represented an 0. These cards were then fed into another machine, known as a card-reader, that was attached to the computer.

This two-stage process took some time. Nowadays, a wide range of input devices can feed information of various kinds straight into the computer. For words and numbers, the most widely used device is a keyboard like the one shown above, with keys arranged like a typewriter. However, even a fast typist cannot hope to keep up with a computer's pace, and it is all too easy for humans to make mistakes.

It might be more convenient if we could simply tell the computer what to do. Unfortunately, it is very difficult to make a device that will turn spoken instructions into binary numbers. People have 'voice-prints' that are as individual as their finger-prints. So at present, **voice recognition** units can only 'recognize' a limited number of words.

Graphics tablets allow shapes like maps to be

Above: Graphics tablets allow shapes to be copied directly into a computer.

'traced' with a 'pen' and loaded directly into the computer. The tablet is sensitive and can follow the movement of the pen. It turns the shape into electrical impulses which the computer can process.

Other devices can convert temperature and pressure readings into digital form. They allow computers to control robots and production processes. Still others can decode information from telephone lines and television broadcasts.

Above: In the future, speaking information into a computer may become more common.

Memory

We use different kinds of memory for different purposes. Short-term memory is useful when we need to remember something for a short period. After looking up a phone number, you only need to remember it for long enough to dial it. Long-term memory is essential for facts and skills that we use a lot, like the alphabet or how to multiply. But our memories are limited, so we back them up with external memory stores, like libraries.

Computers also store information externally as well as inside themselves.

Internal memory

A computer's internal memory is of two kinds; RAM and ROM. **Random Access Memory (RAM)** is the computer's short-term working-space. During its working life, a computer's RAM may be 'overwritten' with new programs and data thousands or millions of times.

Read Only Memory (ROM) can only be 'read' from, it cannot be 'written on'. It is used to store software which will always be needed. ROM software is a permanent part of the machine, unlike RAM, which is 'forgotten' when the computer is switched off.

Comparing a computer system with a home hi-fi system again, ROM resembles a record disc that can only be played, not recorded. RAM is more like a blank cassette tape which can be recorded, wiped clean, and recorded again. However, the computer can get to, or 'access', any part of its RAM 'at random'. In this way it is quite unlike a cassette tape, which has to be played through from the beginning in order to find a particular piece.

A computer has two types of internal memory, both RAM and ROM, and also external memory.

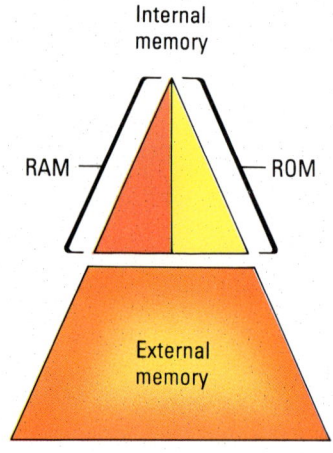

Internal memory

RAM — ROM

External memory

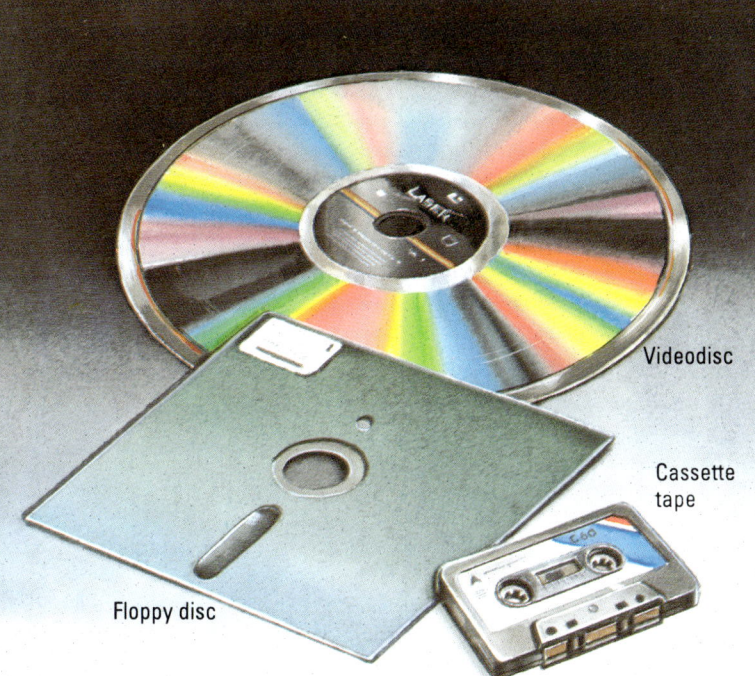

Videodisc

Cassette tape

Floppy disc

External memory

Oddly enough, ordinary audio cassette tapes can be used as external memory for computers. They are not 'random-access' of course, and this makes them slow to use. But cassette tapes and recorders are cheap and widespread, and many home computers depend on them.

'Floppy' discs are another way of storing external memory. They are like very flimsy 45 rpm records, and are easily damaged. Discs can be accessed at random, so loading a program takes

External memory can be stored in a number of different forms. Cassettes and floppy discs are the most common, at present.

seconds rather than minutes. They need a special **disc drive** to 'read' and 'write' the information on them, however, and this can be expensive to buy.

In the future, **videodiscs** may be used as external memory. They are easier to handle than floppy discs and can hold an enormous amount of information.

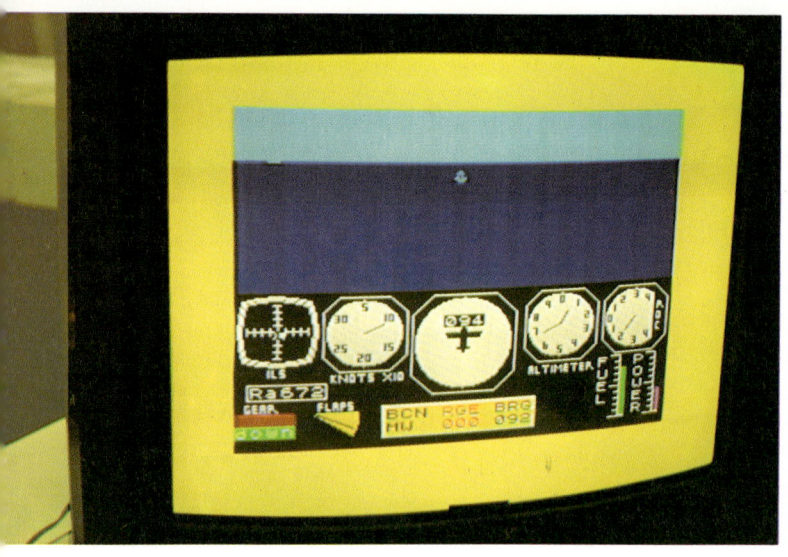

Output Devices

No matter how clever a computer is at processing information, it is of little use unless the output is produced in a suitable form. Most modern computers can send information to a number of different output devices at once.

The two most important, at present, are the screen and the **printer**. Screens can **display** words and numbers, and also pictures, known as **graphics**, as shown above. Many microcomputers can be connected to ordinary domestic televisions – colour or black-and-white. However, special **monitors** give even better results.

Screens are fine for immediate results, but in most cases we still need to have a permanent record of the computer's work. After all, the screen goes blank when you switch off, and although you can store output on floppy discs, it is not much use if the person you want to communicate with hasn't got a disc drive. So most serious users still regard a printer as essential to record the output on paper.

Computer printers

Printers vary enormously in cost, quality and speed. Small computers are usually used with dot-matrix printers, which form each letter or number from a pattern of dots. If you look closely at a computerized till receipt, you will probably be able to see the dots. The patterns of dots can also be rearranged to print graphics.

For high-quality printing, which looks like it has been typed by a good electric typewriter, a different method is used. The letters and symbols are arranged on a rotating 'daisy-wheel'. Daisy-wheel printers are more expensive, however.

Computer sound

Many computers also produce some kind of sound output. Beeps and hoots can be used to attract the user's attention to an error, or to signal the need to load some data – or just for fun.

Some computers can also manufacture music and speech, using special synthesizers. The quality varies enormously, and some synthesized speech sounds peculiar. But speech output is already very useful for the blind, or people who have to watch other instruments.

Simultaneous output of music in sound, on the screen and from the printer.

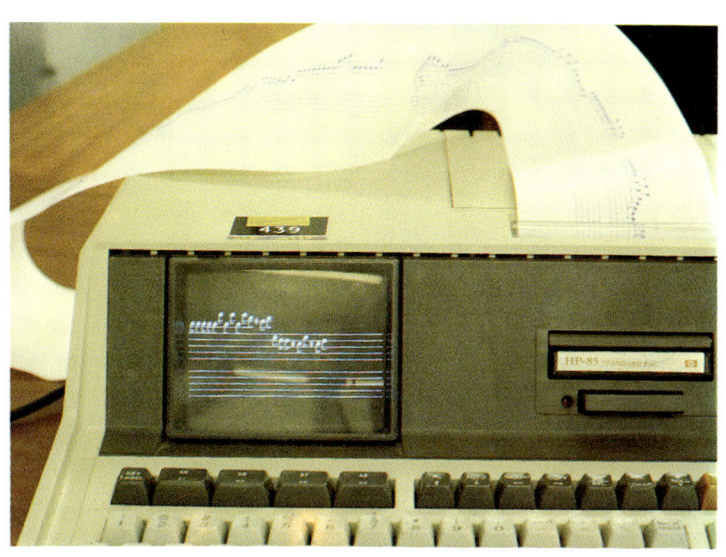

Graphics

Graphic output is not only useful for computer games. It serves an important purpose when computers are put to work in design, education and engineering.

Resolution is a measure of the fineness of the lines that can be drawn on the screen. 'Low resolution' graphics divide the screen into about 40 squares across by about 20 down. The computer can then build up pictures by blocking in some of the squares. The 'squares' are called **pixels** (picture cells). Low resolution is good enough for bar charts and simple diagrams, but curves need 'medium resolution' (about 300 pixels across by 200 down).

Accurate maps and drawings need 'high resolution', which means at least 500 by 500 pixels have to be controlled separately. This uses a lot of processing power and memory – more than most ordinary microcomputers can manage.

Animated graphics are moving images. Animation can be produced quite easily on many computers, and works very well in educational programs and games.

From top to bottom: low, medium and high resolution graphics.

Combine this with three-dimensional effects and high resolution, and lifelike images can be made to move and rotate on the screen.

The drawings above were produced using special graphics software. To do this, a computer needs a large memory to control the screen display and a lot of processing power to work out what the object looks like from different angles. The program can also show cut-away views of the object.

A Complete System

A processor on its own is of little use. It is only as part of a complete **system** with input, output, external memory and the right sort of software that the computer can do anything useful.

Suppose that the girl shown above is using the computer to study how people travel in a town. She starts by loading her program and data from a floppy disc. Within seconds, it has been copied into the computer's RAM.

As soon as she types "RUN" on the keyboard, the program sends a message to the screen asking her what area she has been studying. She types in the right area code at the keyboard, and then sets up the graphics tablet with a street map showing exactly where she collected her data, such as the number of buses in the area. Once she has fed in her data, the program updates the information it has been given on previous occasions. Then it works out the passenger distances travelled by different methods of transport and shows this on the screen.

She can choose to see the results on a map or as a table of figures. Both can be printed out so she can take the results away with her. Before she switches off, the program reminds her to 'save' her results onto the disc. Otherwise, her results would be lost.

A computer network

It is rather wasteful to have a lot of equipment just for one person to use for the odd ten minutes. A computer **network** allows others to feed their data and programs into the computer at the same time. Each user needs a keyboard for input and a screen for output, but they can share items like printers and external memory, which they only use occasionally.

The control computer has special network software which sorts out which user 'station' should get priority. For example, a request to load a new program usually takes priority over asking for a print-out of results. Networks are very useful in schools and offices, as they allow more people to use the same computer system.

In a network, a computer can share its processing power, memory and printer among many user 'stations'.

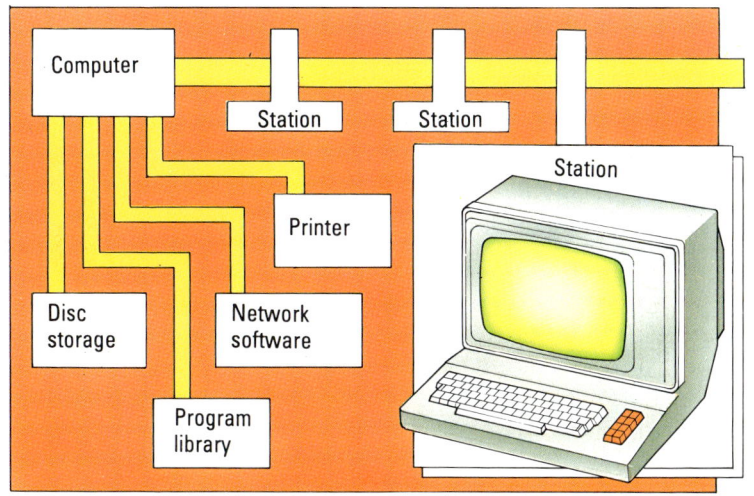

With suitable input and output devices, a general-purpose computer can process many different kinds of input and produce output in a variety of forms.

A true computer is always general-purpose. Although we may talk of 'computers' in video games or vacuum cleaners, actually what they have is a **dedicated** microprocessor chip. This type of chip can only do one job – the one it was programmed to do when it was made; it is hardly a real computer.

For example, the processor in a washing machine is no good for anything except controlling wash cycles. Its input is the settings fed in by the user and the signals fed back from the timer or temperature sensor. It needs little memory, and its calculations result in simple output – control messages to the timing device and water heater.

The strength of a real computer is its flexibility. It can deal with input of different kinds, can run any kind of software, and can produce output in a variety of forms. This might mean controlling a robot, drawing a picture, playing a tune or printing out a report.

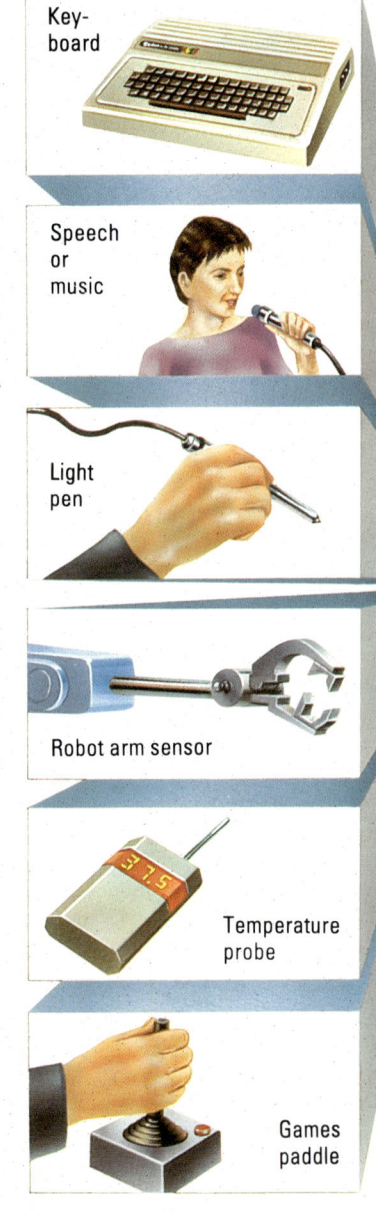

Keyboard

Speech or music

Light pen

Robot arm sensor

Temperature probe

Games paddle

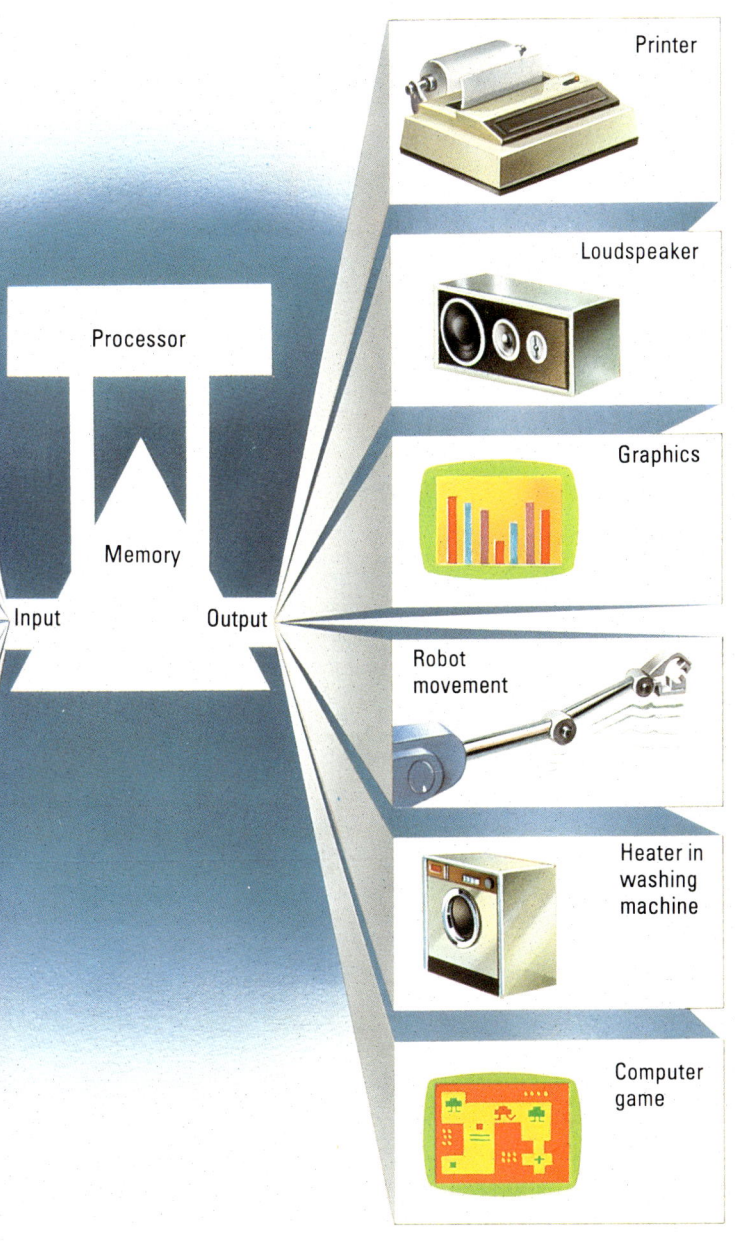

Processor

Memory

Input

Output

Printer

Loudspeaker

Graphics

Robot movement

Heater in washing machine

Computer game

41

How Does it Work?

A flow chart helps to plan the main stages of a program, but it has to be turned into detailed instructions for the computer to obey. Programs are written in a special **programming language**, which the computer then translates into its own binary language. There are many different programming languages (see pages 74-75). The one shown here is called **BASIC**.

Times table tester

Suppose you wanted to test yourself on your multiplication tables. A computer could be programmed to pick random numbers so the sums will be different each time. For each sum, it could work out the right answer, compare it with the one you type in and print a suitable comment. The screen on this page shows the sort of 'conversation' you would have with the computer while the program is running.

Above it is the flow chart, with an actual program opposite. BASIC programs are written in numbered lines, so the flow chart has also been numbered to help you to see how it works.

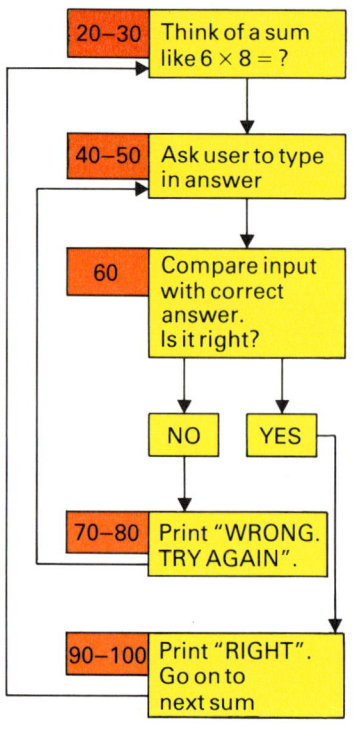

20–30	Think of a sum like 6 × 8 = ?
40–50	Ask user to type in answer
60	Compare input with correct answer. Is it right?
	NO / YES
70–80	Print "WRONG. TRY AGAIN".
90–100	Print "RIGHT". Go on to next sum

What is 6 times 8?
?42
Wrong. Try again
What is 6 times 8?
?48
Right
What is 4 times 3?
?12
Right

'TABLES' PROGRAM   COMMENTS

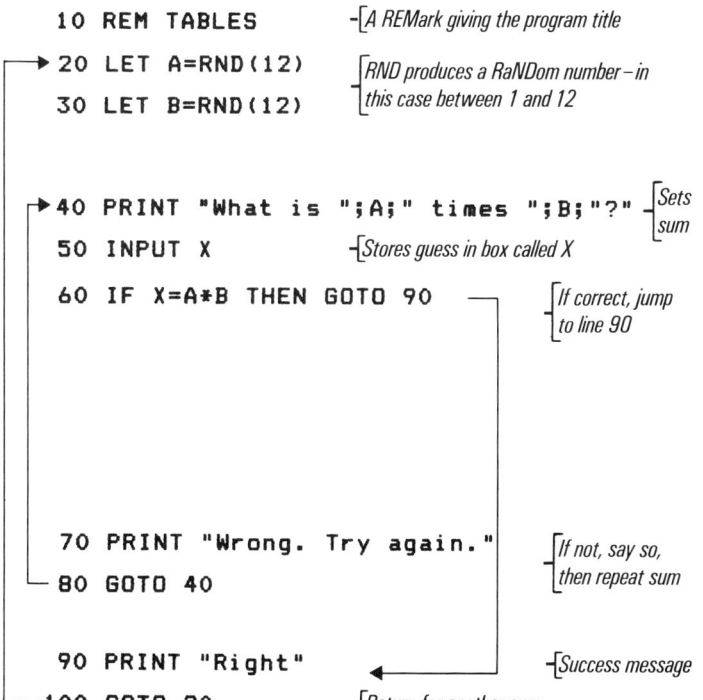

```
 10 REM TABLES
 20 LET A=RND(12)
 30 LET B=RND(12)

 40 PRINT "What is ";A;" times ";B;"?"
 50 INPUT X
 60 IF X=A*B THEN GOTO 90




 70 PRINT "Wrong. Try again."
 80 GOTO 40

 90 PRINT "Right"
100 GOTO 20
```

-[A REMark giving the program title

[RND produces a RaNDom number – in
[this case between 1 and 12

-[Sets sum

-[Stores guess in box called X

[If correct, jump to line 90

[If not, say so, then repeat sum

-[Success message

-[Return for another sum

BASIC words look like English, but have special meanings. REM tells the computer to ignore the rest of that line. PRINT makes it write on the screen whatever follows between "quotation marks". PRINT ;A; means write the number stored in A, but not on a new line. INPUT means take whatever is put in at the keyboard and store it. A*B means multiply the number in A times the one stored in B. GOTO means jump to the line number given.

The program above is written in BBC BASIC; there are lots of other kinds, or **dialects**, of BASIC. Here, RND picks a number at random; other dialects use RND in a different way.

Hunt the Hurkle

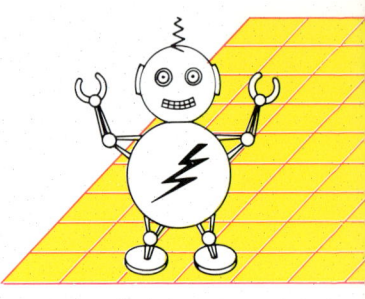

Let's look at a more interesting program which uses the same basic idea. The Hurkle is a shy animal which is hiding in an area 9 units square. To hunt the Hurkle, you type in a pair of numbers like 6,8. The program then checks whether the Hurkle is anywhere in the square 6 units East and 8 units North of the bottom left corner (see second diagram on page 45).

The program below is based on a flow-chart like the one on page 42. The diagrams opposite show how the program was thought out. You would not see the diagrams on your screen.

'HURKLE1' PROGRAM WITH COMMENTS

```
10 REM HURKLE1
```
A REMark simply gives a message to the user – in this case the program title

```
20 LET E=RND(9)
30 LET N=RND(9)
```
Hides Hurkle in a RaNDom position between numbers 1 and 9

```
40 PRINT "Type your guess"
```
Tells user what to do

```
50 INPUT X,Y
```
Puts user's guess in boxes called X and Y

```
60 IF X=E AND Y=N THEN GOTO 90
```
Checks if Hurkle found

```
80 GOTO 40
```
If not found jump to line 40 for another try

```
90 PRINT "Well done!"
95 PRINT "You found the Hurkle"
100 END
```
Success message

44

First the Hurkle must be hidden at random; let's call its position E,N. E is short for Easting – the number which says how far East the Hurkle is. N is short for Northing. RND(9) picks a random number between 1 and 9:

```
LET E=RND(9)
LET N=RND(9)
```

Now, using a PRINT instruction, a message must be sent to the screen to tell the player to make a guess. Once the player types in the pair of numbers, the INPUT instruction stores the Easting in a 'box' called X, and the Northing in one called Y:

```
PRINT "Type your guess"
INPUT X,Y
```

The program must compare the player's guess (X,Y) with the Hurkle's position (E,N). If both are equal, the Hurkle has been found and the program jumps to line 90:

```
IF X=E AND Y=N THEN GOTO 90
```

If the guess is wrong, the program must jump back to line 40 to let the player have another go. The program will go round and round this **loop** until the guess is right:

```
GOTO 40
```

Line 90 is the final bit of the program which makes a success message appear on the screen:

```
PRINT "Well done!"
```

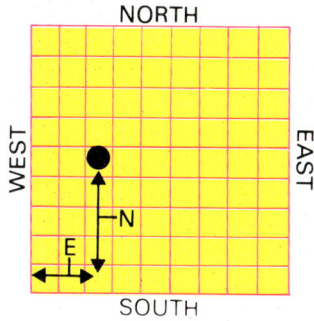

The Hurkle is at 3,5.

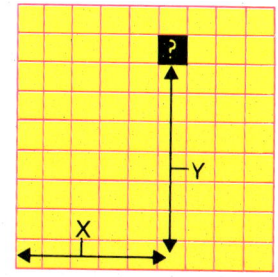

The player's guess is 6,8.

```
PRINT "You found the Hurkle"
END
```

To complete this program, we just have to add the first line which gives the title (HURKLE1) and the line numbers. BASIC programs are often numbered in tens to leave plenty of space to add extra instruction lines later on without having to renumber everything. The computer just obeys the instructions in numerical order. It doesn't matter how the numbers are spaced out.

With HURKLE1 the player has no way of knowing where the Hurkle is – apart from blind guesswork! A better program would give clues about which direction to move in after each guess. The directional clues would help the player to work towards the Hurkle's position.

The clues can be added to the HURKLE1 program between lines 60 and 80. The flow chart below gives a summary of how HURKLE2 would work.

```
Type your guess
?6,8
Type your guess
?1,2
Type your guess
?4,6
Type your guess
?3,5
Well done!
You found the Hurkle
```

Above: HURKLE1 in action. The player was just lucky to find the Hurkle so quickly.

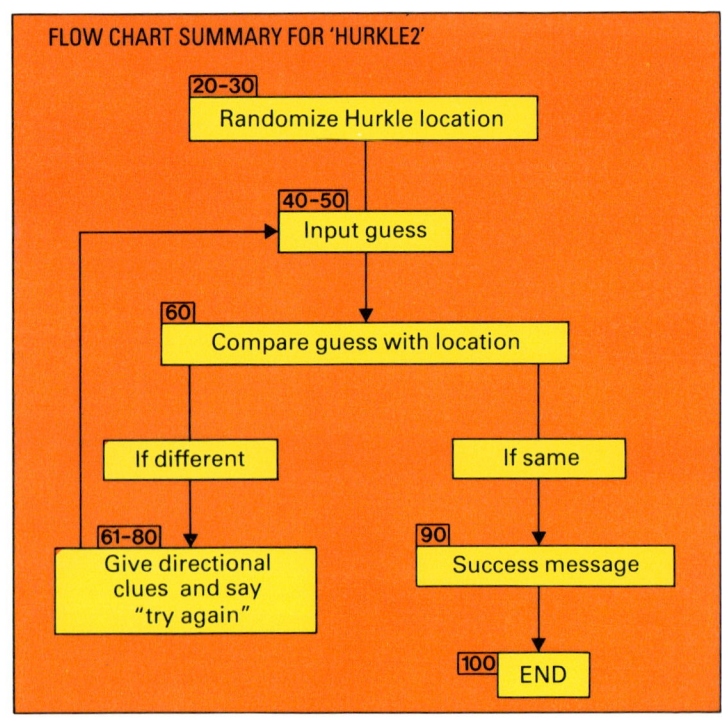

FLOW CHART SUMMARY FOR 'HURKLE2'

20-30 Randomize Hurkle location

40-50 Input guess

60 Compare guess with location

If different

If same

61-80 Give directional clues and say "try again"

90 Success message

100 END

HURKLE2 directions

Working out how to write the clues section of the program takes a bit of thought. The flow chart and program for this are shown on page 48. However, you could try to rough out a flow chart for how the clues would work before you turn over.

Each clue consists of a message to go in a particular direction. Although "Go NorthEast" looks as if it came from a single PRINT instruction, it is actually built up from three parts: "Go ", "North" and "East". All clues start with the PRINT instruction "Go ". Some are followed by a simple direction like "North" or "East". Others need a combined one like "NorthEast" or "SouthWest".

Because we always say "Go NorthEast" rather than "Go EastNorth", the program sorts out whether the Northing is right before it looks at the Easting. However, the guess is always typed in the opposite way – Eastings are *always* put in before Northings.

Starting with the Northing, then, the program first checks if this half of the guess is correct. (If it is, it jumps to the part which looks at the Easting.) If the

Type your guess
?1,2
Go NorthEast
?6,7
Go East
?9,7
Go West
?8,7
Well done!
You found the Hurkle

Above: What appears on the screen when HURKLE2 is running.

Northing is *not* equal to the Hurkle's, the program tests whether the number is too large or too small. If the guess is too far South, the clue must say "Go North". Otherwise, the program must jump to a bit telling the player to "Go South".

Next, the Easting is looked at in the same sort of way to produce clues saying "Go East" or "Go West". Then the program returns to the line which inputs the player's next guess.

When looking at page 48, remember that the program only goes through the clue section if the guess is wrong. If both Easting and Northing are correct, the program jumps straight to the success message and ends.

The flow chart below shows how the directional clues are built up. Lines 20 to 60, and 90 to 100 of HURKLE2 are exactly the same as in HURKLE1. The semi-colons in lines 64 and 66 allow the clues to be shown as combined ones if necessary. Otherwise, every PRINT instruction creates a new line. Line 72 simply makes a blank line on the screen before the next guess.

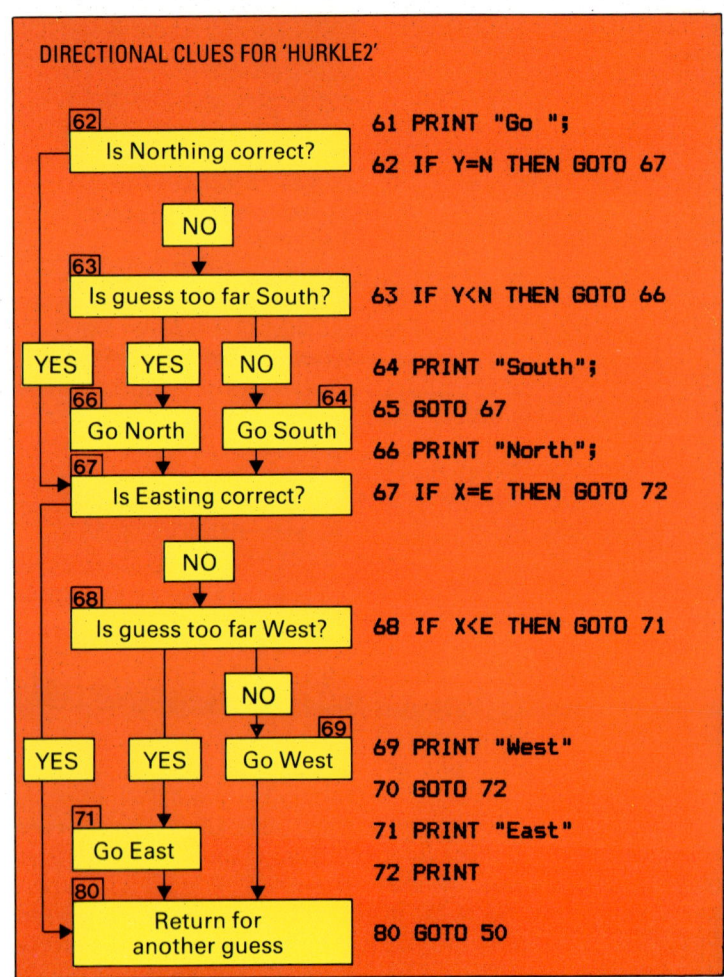

DIRECTIONAL CLUES FOR 'HURKLE2'

Flow chart	Code
62 Is Northing correct?	61 PRINT "Go ";
	62 IF Y=N THEN GOTO 67
NO	
63 Is guess too far South?	63 IF Y<N THEN GOTO 66
YES / YES / NO	64 PRINT "South";
66 Go North / **64** Go South	65 GOTO 67
	66 PRINT "North";
67 Is Easting correct?	67 IF X=E THEN GOTO 72
NO	
68 Is guess too far West?	68 IF X<E THEN GOTO 71
NO	
YES / YES / **69** Go West	69 PRINT "West"
	70 GOTO 72
71 Go East	71 PRINT "East"
	72 PRINT
80 Return for another guess	80 GOTO 50

Beyond HURKLE2

HURKLE2 is a much better game than HURKLE1, but there is still room for improvement. A player might take ages to finish the program. One way around this would be to give the player a limited number of guesses – say five. By keeping track of how many guesses have been used, the program could print a suitable message if the Hurkle is found quickly, or else stop the game after five guesses.

FOR . . . NEXT loops

Many programs make use of loops – sections of programs that are obeyed over and over again. In HURKLE3, the letter K is used as a counter in a FOR . . . NEXT loop. K is set to 1 for the first guess, 2 for the second guess, and so on. The lines:
FOR K=1 TO 5
followed later by:
NEXT K
make the program repeat all the instructions in between these lines, increasing the *value* of K by 1 each time.

The program will go on until the player has either found the Hurkle or else used up the 5 guesses. Each time it goes round the loop, the program will print in turn "Type guess 1", "Type

Type guess 1
?5,5
Go SouthWest
Type guess 2
?2,2
Well done!
You found it in 2 guesses
Another game?
?Y
The Hurkle hides again:
Type guess 1

Above: HURKLE3 in action. This program keeps track of the number of guesses.

guess 2" and so on, up to "Type guess 5". The final message also makes use of the K counter by printing things like "Well done! You found it in 3 guesses".

HURKLE3 can also offer the player another game. GET$ makes the program search through whatever is typed in reply. If the instruction asks if GET$=N, the program will look for the letter 'N' (as in 'Not likely'). So the line: IF GET$=N THEN GOTO 100 will make the program jump to the END line. Otherwise, it will set up a new Hurkle.

The HURKLE3 program is shown on page 70. If you can follow how it works, you are on the way to understanding programming.

Computers in Use

If a sudden fault made all the computers in the world go wrong, there would be immediate chaos in banks and airlines. Some hospital patients would die without computers to monitor them. Offices and factories would close down, and millions of people would lose their jobs.

If you walk down a main shopping street, you can see how widespread computers have become. You might even see one sitting in a shop window. Or you might notice someone using a terminal which links up to a computer some distance away. Travel agents, for example, are often linked to the airlines' computers so they can get instant information.

Many shop goods already carry **bar codes**. The spacing between the bars carries a code which identifies the product and its price. Some supermarket check-outs use a special device that can 'read' this code. It automatically produces a detailed receipt for the shopper, and can store the information so that the shop-keeper can tell when his stock gets low.

Computers help travel agents with instant information. Bookings are made at the press of a button.

Cash by computer

Most banks now hold their records on a central computer and give customers 24-hour access to their money through a special cash card that has a secret 'Personal Identification Number', or PIN. The card can be used at any of the bank's 'cash dispensers' – computer terminals with built-in screens, printers and cash counters. A card owner puts her card into the machine and types in her PIN. First, the machine checks that she has given the right number. If the PIN is correct, the machine then makes sure that she has enough money in her bank account, before counting out the cash and presenting it to her.

Above: A bank's cash dispenser.

Below: At a supermarket, a special scanner 'reads' the black bar code printed on each item.

Distance No Object

With the correct linking equipment, information and software from a central computer can be sent over vast distances, and displayed on ordinary television sets in homes and offices.

Teletext systems code information and then broadcast it as part of a normal television signal. Any television set can display teletext information once it has been decoded; 'teletext televisions' are simply sets with **decoders** built into them. Teletext can provide news

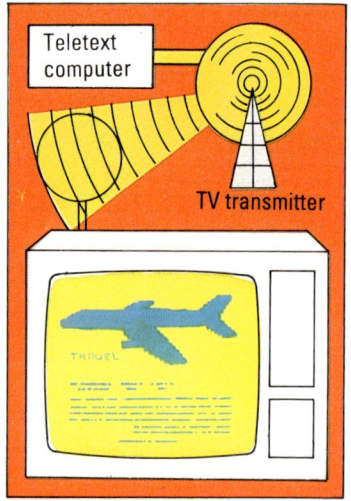

Teletext computer

TV transmitter

TRAVEL

Prestel computer

Telephone exchange

The Prestel computer sends information down telephone lines onto TV screens. You can select the information you want, and ask the computer questions about it.

Left: Teletext uses ordinary television signals to broadcast information.

Above: Cyclops allows users to exchange information on TV screens over a distance.

and travel information, for example. It can also send out **telesoftware** – computer programs that can be loaded straight into the memory of another computer.

Unlike teletext, **Prestel** users can send messages to the computer as well as receive them. By dialling a special telephone number, users can connect with the Prestel computer, which stores vast amounts of news, travel and shopping data.

By pressing keys on a hand-held keypad, you can choose the information you want to read. It is then sent down the phone lines onto your television screen. The keypad can also be used to order goods, book holidays, and play quiz games.

Cyclops was designed for use in education. It uses both telephone and television screen. In addition, it has a special unit for storing pictures on tape cassettes. Using a special 'pen', one person can draw a picture which appears on his TV screen. The person at the other end of the telephone sees the same picture on her TV screen. She can add to the picture, rub bits out and redraw them and talk about it over the phone.

Without computers, we could not launch satellites into space, or keep track of their movements.

Transport and Space

Modern transport depends heavily on computers. Big car companies use computers to pay wages and order supplies. Computers also help designers to improve car body shapes. The computer's ability to produce drawings in three dimensions (see page 36) means that a program can be written to test a car's shape for things like wind resistance before it is built.

Airlines use computers to store reservations and issue tickets, and also for cargo control. Computers help pilots to fly their aircraft, to navigate, and to control the fuel supply and wing flaps. Most of the time, commercial planes fly under computer controlled 'automatic pilots'. Human pilots take over only when the plane takes off and lands.

Computers also control the complicated 'simulators' used in pilot training. These machines create highly realistic scenes of a pilot's cockpit as a plane comes in to land, for example. So trainee pilots can gain experience of hundreds of landings without risking human lives or expensive planes.

Air traffic controllers use computers to help them direct incoming and outgoing flights.

Computers and space

The space race has also been a computer race. From the start, computers have been used to guide rockets and satellites. On-board computers can make split-second decisions about mid-course corrections; they can control 'soft' landings on planets, and guide robot explorers.

Back on Earth, larger computers at the Mission Control centres keep track of what the spacecraft are doing, and help to process the information sent back from space. Fuzzy satellite photographs, for example, can be made clear and sharp by computer processing.

Computers in the Classroom

Computers never get impatient, which is one reason why they are good at helping people to learn. Sitting at a separate terminal, each pupil is able to work at the speed that is best for him or her. Simple programs, like the one on page 43, can be used with a whole class of pupils, leaving the teacher free to help individuals with their problems.

With good graphics and sound effects, computers can be programmed to deal with almost any subject. Pupils can compose music, draw in colour and carry out dangerous scientific experiments – all while sitting at a school computer. Also, computer games, like the Animal Game shown opposite, make learning fun.

Robot 'toys' that can be programmed help pupils to learn how to control computers and to use programming languages. Such skills are not only useful for those who want to work with computers. Nowadays, learning to control a computer is as vital as knowing how to read and write.

The Animal Game

ANIMAL is a game in which the pupil teaches the computer, not the other way around. The player chooses an animal and the program tries to guess what the animal is. If it fails, it asks for a question that will help it to guess the animal next time. Every time it plays, the program adds more animals to its memory.

On the right, you can see how the screen might look when ANIMAL is being played. This program started by 'knowing' only three animals that live in water: plaice, haddock and trout. Next time, the program will 'know' a fourth animal, and have 'learned' one way of telling the difference between a whale and the other three. But if the next player happens to like whale and chips for supper, it will be foiled again!

In order to teach the computer, the player first has to find out about the animal she has chosen. She then has to think up good questions to give the computer. When a whole classroom of pupils play this game they are also learning about animals from each other, by seeing the questions the computer has been given.

Above: Microchips are used in educational 'toys'. These two both have electronic speech; one tests your tables, the other your spelling.

Below: ANIMAL on screen.

Have you chosen an animal?
YES
Does it live in water?
YES
Has it got 5 letters?
YES
Is it a trout?
NO
I give up. What is it?
WHALE
Tell me a question to distinguish WHALE from TROUT.
WOULD YOU EAT IT WITH CHIPS?
What is the answer for WHALE?
NO

The Brains of a Robot

Robots differ from other automatic machines in that they can be programmed to carry out a variety of jobs, instead of mindlessly repeating the same movement for ever. This is because each robot has a computer 'brain'.

'Teaching' a robot
A robot has to be taught each job by a human operator, who takes the robot through every movement, step-by-step, until the task is completed. The operator checks that each movement is exactly right before pressing a 'record' button to store it in the robot's computer memory. Alternatively, the operator can hold the robot arm and guide it smoothly through the complete set of movements, which is stored as a single 'program'.

Below: A skilled worker guides a robot arm through the movements needed to spray an object with an even coat of paint.

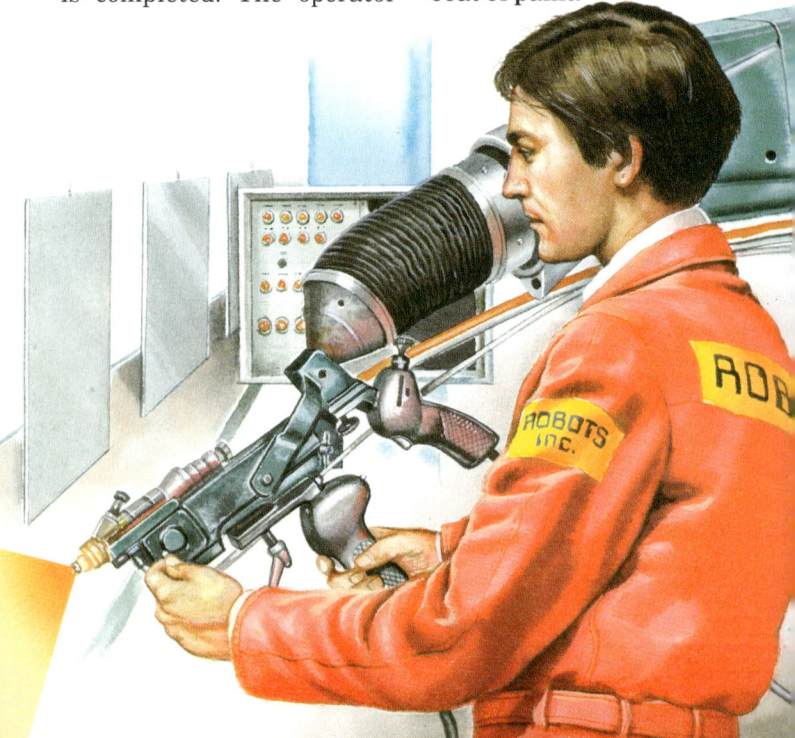

Robots as workers

Most of the world's robots work in factories. They do very routine jobs, like assembling parts, spray-painting and welding. Unlike humans, robots don't need protection from poisonous chemicals, noise or high temperatures, and they never get bored or need to sleep. However, robots are limited in the work they can do, and cannot easily move around. It is usually necessary to reorganize how the work is done to make things easy for the robot.

Many people fear that robots will make unemployment worse, and oppose

Above: Robots assemble Mini Metro cars as they move along the production line in a factory.

their use, even for boring and dangerous jobs. Others believe that, with good management, robots could make enough wealth for humans to do more interesting jobs or have more leisure time.

In the future, robots will be smaller and more mobile. They will be able to obey simple spoken instructions and do a wider range of jobs. Probably they will be able to 'see' and 'feel' their way, using built-in video cameras and touch sensors.

Computers and Crime

Computers are changing the nature of crime and criminals. As credit cards and computerized bank drafts become more widely accepted, less cash will be carried around. There will be less point in 'wages snatches'. Of course, credit cards can be stolen, too, but then the thief has to forge the signature of the rightful owner in order to buy anything.

Many motoring crimes could even be prevented altogether by computer control of car engines. For example, speeding, car theft and driving while drunk or uninsured could all be made impossible if suitable controls were built into the car engine and dashboard (though many people would resist such changes). However, computers can also be used to commit crimes.

The 'Salami' fraud

One common type of computer crime is called the 'Salami' technique because the money comes in 'thin slices' from lots of customers' accounts. It works by collecting the tiny percentages of a penny that are often left over after a calculation, but are too small to show in the account statements.

In an honest system, these fractions are shared out among all the customers. But in a complicated program, it is easy to bury a coded instruction which siphons off the tiny fractions into just one account, belonging to an accomplice. Sometimes the money is allowed to build up and then sent to another country. In this way, the criminals can steal enormous sums of money over a few years!

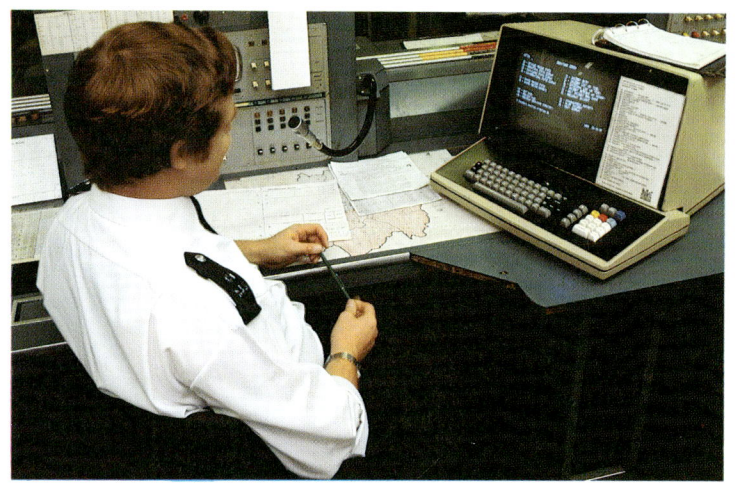

Caught by computer!

Computers help the police as well as the criminals. In many countries, details of the registered owners of all cars are stored on a central computer. A police officer can radio through to headquarters with the licence-plate number of a suspect car and get back the name and address of the real owner within seconds. Armed with this information, he can stop the car and find out if the driver is a thief.

Computers can help in other ways as well. A violent crime was committed in Utah in America, but there were no witnesses. A passing helicopter had been taking aerial photographs, but the suspect was hardly

Above: A modern police force depends on computers for fast and accurate information.

visible. After computer processing, the photograph was made so much larger and clearer that experts were able to work out the attacker's height, sleeve length and shoe size! Their figures were accurate enough to lead to a conviction.

Detection is helped by vast 'data banks', stored in police computers. In some countries, millions of criminal fingerprints are held on a videotape system linked to a computer. The program can search through the entire collection in seconds to find matching sets of prints.

Microfuture

In the future, even more computing power will be packed onto a single chip. As a result, computers will be smaller and more portable. Also, software will become simpler to use and easier to transfer from one computer to another.

Micros on the move

Voice and handwritten input will make the keyboard a rarity, and paper will be used very sparingly. Very little power will be needed, so most computers will operate on solar-powered batteries. Computers will not be limited to specialists who work for large organizations. Ordinary people of all ages will rely on them for everyday needs. For example, the wristwatch micro will develop into a personal assistant, giving reminders, taking notes and acting as a telephone.

Almost everyone, from teenagers upward, will be able to use an electronic car for short-range personal transport. These will have so many built-in safety devices they will almost drive themselves, and finding the way around will be child's play with the video screen homing device.

Below left: The car of the future will have dashboard displays to warn of hazards and malfunctions, and automatic settings to control speed and conserve fuel. A voice recognition unit will make it impossible for unauthorized people to use the car.

Below: The wristwatch micro will be cheap and flexible. Voice output will give the time, date and reminders. A tiny microphone will pick up dictated instructions and a display screen will allow the watch to be used with the speaker turned off.

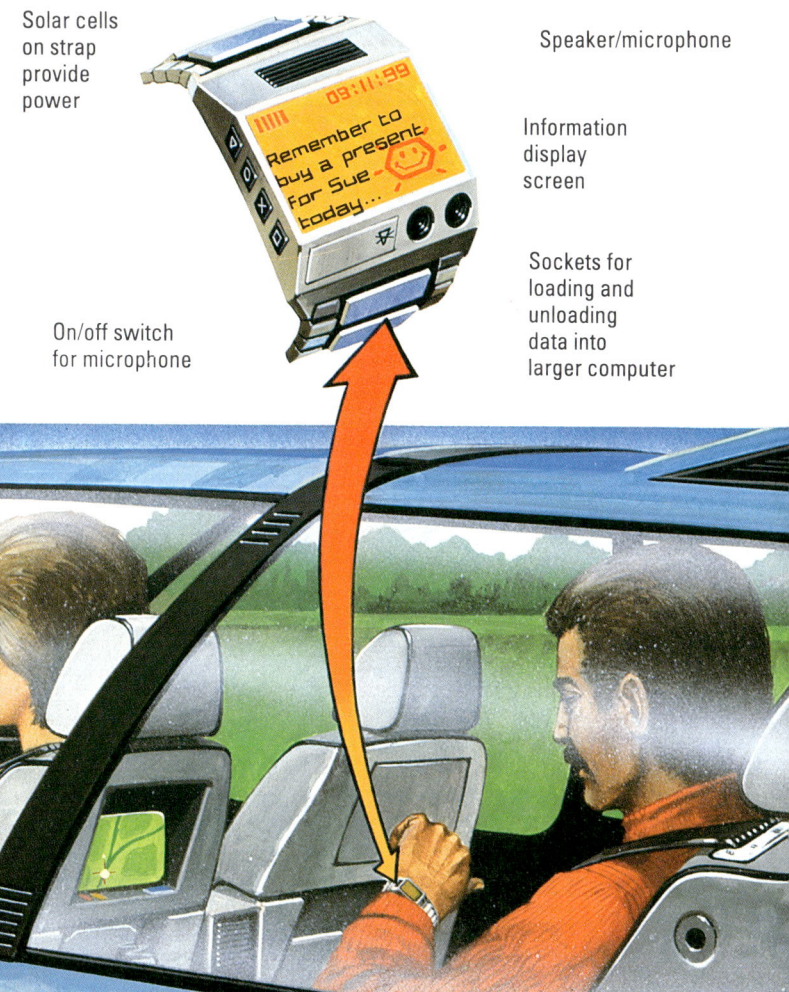

Solar cells on strap provide power

Speaker/microphone

Information display screen

On/off switch for microphone

Sockets for loading and unloading data into larger computer

09:11:99

Remember to buy a present for Sue today...

Electronic Life

Computers will supply many of people's needs in their own homes. Fewer people will want, or need, to live in big cities in order to commute to their work. Home computers will allow many people to work from their homes. Much routine factory and farm work will be done by robots. Working hours will be shorter, holidays and leisure hours longer. More people will have active hobbies, like sports, gardening and music.

The schools of the future

Home computers will mean that all the knowledge of the world's great libraries will be available to everyone. Advanced software will bring this knowledge to life with sound, colour and animated graphics.

Faced with this challenge, schools will have to adapt to survive. Perhaps they will concentrate on 'live' teaching in areas where electronic education cannot compete. For example, young children may attend nearby 'schools' for play. Older children may be allowed to choose whether and when to go to school.

A family scene

Shown above is a living-room of the future. Built into one wall is a flat display screen and computer console with loudspeakers, colour printer, videodisc storage and a telecommunications centre. Sockets allow portable micros to receive software and to dump data which can be printed out, processed, or transmitted.

The man is learning to play the guitar. His video-disc contains teaching material and expert demonstrations; his own efforts will be recorded and transmitted to a teacher for comments. Meanwhile, his children are playing a space exploration game, which has realistic graphics. Like most of their lessons and games, this was loaded into their micro from the home computer console.

Their mother is at work on an industrial magazine that she edits. If she wants to discuss an illustration with her designer 300 kilometres away, she just plugs the telephone into her desk-top micro. When the magazine is ready, it is printed out in the homes of subscribers, and the bill for it is sent automatically.

Global Village

How will human beings react to the possibilities and problems brought by computers? Will people sit at home amid their electronic gadgets, not caring about the rest of the world? Or will they use their time and equipment to communicate with, and learn more about, people in other countries?

World citizens?
Electronic mail by satellite is already being used by businesses who can afford it. In the future it will be cheaper and available to more people. Combined with limited computer translation between languages, it could transform our ability to exchange information with people on other continents.

In one sense, it could be easier than before for the developed nations to share their technological success with the rest of the world. Cheap, portable computers are useful in all kinds of situations, and they could be easily available to all countries. But each country will have to decide if computers are a good thing for them.

Left: A doctor attending a disaster uses her briefcase micro to find blood supplies and to confirm her diagnosis.

The computer revolution

In the last century, the industrial revolution achieved remarkable technological progress, but it also created terrible working conditions for many people. The computer revolution is only just beginning, but its effects may be even greater.

Computers offer many new opportunities, but only humans can decide how they should be used. On the one hand, computers can make weapons ever more deadly and these could be used to destroy our civilization. On the other hand, they could improve communications between people of different continents, and help to build world peace and understanding.

Below: In the future, computer-controlled laser satellites could make instant, world-wide communication more widely available.

Further Facts

Computer Firsts

Over a century ago, a famous man and a remarkable woman discovered the principles of computer hardware and software. Charles Babbage invented the Analytical Engine, the world's first programmable computer. It was never built, but he wrote detailed letters about it to Ada Augusta, Lord Byron's daughter. She saw its potential and described how software would work.

These ideas were ahead of their time, however, and working computers had to wait until electronics arrived in the 1940s. Since then, progress has been breathtaking; first with the discovery of transistors, then of silicon chips, which carry an ever-increasing number of parts each year.

It is hard for us to grasp the effects of such rapid change. The chart opposite shows that most of the progress happened within the last fifty years. What it cannot really display is how the *pace* of change has speeded up.

Imagine that the minutes on a clock-face represent the 5000 years for which humans have used counting machines. Each minute stands for about 83 years, so Pascal's adding machine arrived 4 minutes ago, and Babbage's ideas were published about 2 minutes ago. Early computers appeared 30 seconds ago, satellites 20 seconds ago and robots only in the last 10 seconds. Pocket computers, Prestel and telesoftware all arrived in the last few seconds.

3000 BC First abacus, using sand and pebbles

500 BC Chinese abacus, using wires and beads

1643 Pascal's adding machine completed

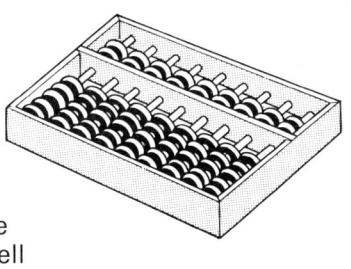

1852 Death of Ada Augusta

1871 Death of Charles Babbage

1876 Telephone patented by Bell

1898 Marconi gives first radio broadcast

1936 BBC gives first television broadcast

1943 Colossus I, high-speed, electronic code-breaking computer, built in Britain

1946 ENIAC, first general-purpose computer, built in USA

1947 BBC starts first public TV service

1948 Transistors discovered

1950 Ferranti Star, first commercial computer

1957 Sputnik I, first satellite, launched from USSR

1959 First integrated circuit produced on silicon chip

1962 First electronic calculators

1964 First word processors

1967 Electronic cash dispensers

1968 Early industrial robots

1970 Electronic pocket calculators

1971 Video recorders

1972 Early video games

1973 First teletext service (ORACLE)

1975 First microcomputers

1977 Videodiscs, and voice recognition

1979 Prestel launched

1980 First pocket computer

1981 Telesoftware available

1982 Hand-held computer terminals

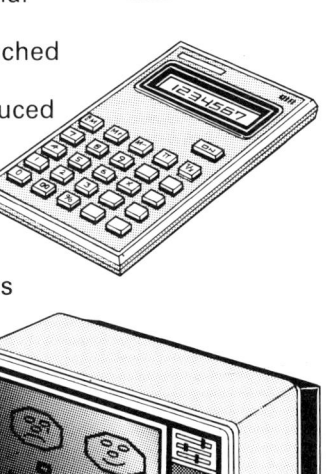

More Programming

Here is one way of writing the program HURKLE3, described on page 49:

```
10 REM HURKLE3
20 LET E=RND(9)
30 LET N=RND(9)
35 FOR K=1 TO 5
40 PRINT "Type guess ";K
50 INPUT X,Y
60 IF X=E AND Y=N THEN GOTO 90
61 PRINT "Go ";
62 IF Y=N THEN GOTO 67
63 IF Y<N THEN GOTO 66
64 PRINT "South";
65 GOTO 67
66 PRINT "North";
67 IF X=E THEN GOTO 72
68 IF X<E THEN GOTO 71
69 PRINT "West"
70 GOTO 72
71 PRINT "East"
72 PRINT
80 NEXT K
81 PRINT
82 PRINT "Sorry, you've had 5 guesses"
83 PRINT "The Hurkle is at ";E;",";N
84 GOTO 96
90 PRINT "Well done!"
95 PRINT "You found it in ";K;" guesses"
96 PRINT "Another game?"
97 IF GET$="N" THEN GOTO 100
98 PRINT "The Hurkle hides again:"
99 GOTO 20
100 END
```

Improve on TABLES

Look back at the TABLES program on page 43. It might give a sum like '11 times 12' to someone who only knew his tables up to 8 times 12. A better program would start by asking the user to type in the highest table he knew. A line saying INPUT H would store his answer in a box called H. The program would then produce sums of the right difficulty, by making A equal to RND(H) instead of RND(12) in line 20.

As it stands, TABLES would run for ever. A counter could make it give, say, 6 sums and then finish. The use of a FOR . . . NEXT loop was explained on page 4S, and is illustrated in lines 35 and 80 of HURKLE3 (shown opposite). In TABLES, the line saying FOR K=1 TO 6 must start the loop before line 20. The line NEXT K ends the loop and the program.

If you have followed all this, try writing out the new program. Line 10 should give the title – TABLES2, for example. Then work out the new lines involving H and K. Lines 30 to 90 should still work as in TABLES, but line 100 will need to be changed.

Then compare your answer with the program shown below.

```
10 REM TABLES2
11 PRINT "What is the highest table
   you know?"
12 INPUT H
13 FOR K=1 TO 6
20 LET A=RND(H)
30 LET B=RND(12)
40 PRINT "What is ";A;" times ";B;"?"
50 INPUT X
60 IF X=A*B THEN GOTO 90
70 PRINT "Wrong. Try again"
80 GOTO 40
90 PRINT "Right"
100 NEXT K
```

TABLES3

Although TABLES2 is better than TABLES, both programs would get stuck in an endless loop if the user kept getting the answer wrong. This could be overcome by adding another counter, W, to keep track of how many wrong answers the user has given.

For example, the program could allow up to 3 wrong answers. Then it could print a message giving the right answer and jump back to set the next sum.

The flow chart opposite shows how this could be done. The box numbers refer to the program lines needed. See if you can follow how the program works. You would only have to add 6 lines to TABLES2:

```
15 LET W=0
61 LET W=W+1
62 IF W<3 THEN GOTO 70
63 PRINT "Sorry, you've had 3 tries"
64 PRINT "Answer is   "; A*B
65 GOTO 100
```

A program to reach the Moon

FOR...NEXT loops make something happen a fixed number of times. RE-PEAT...UNTIL is another kind of loop that repeats a section of the program until some condition is met. Here

'TABLES3' FLOW CHART

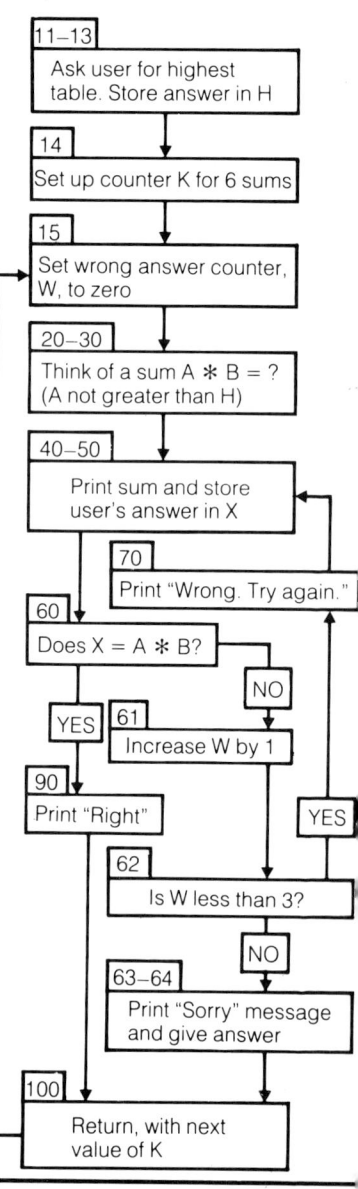

| 11–13 |
| Ask user for highest table. Store answer in H |

| 14 |
| Set up counter K for 6 sums |

| 15 |
| Set wrong answer counter, W, to zero |

| 20–30 |
| Think of a sum A * B = ? (A not greater than H) |

| 40–50 |
| Print sum and store user's answer in X |

| 70 |
| Print "Wrong. Try again." |

| 60 |
| Does X = A * B? |

YES / NO

| 61 |
| Increase W by 1 |

| 90 |
| Print "Right" |

| 62 |
| Is W less than 3? |

YES / NO

| 63–64 |
| Print "Sorry" message and give answer |

| 100 |
| Return, with next value of K |

1·6mm

is a short program that keeps doubling something called T until it gets past 1000:

```
10 LET T=0.1
20 REPEAT
30 LET   T=T*2
40 UNTIL T>1000
```

Try using this idea in a program to find out how many times you would have to fold a piece of paper to reach the Moon. You will need another counter, K=0, to keep track of how many times T is doubled. If you LET K=K+1 inside a loop which REPEATs the doubling UNTIL T is greater than the target, you need only PRINT the final value of K afterwards. The target distance to the Moon is about 384,400 kilometres.

To find a starting value for T, take a sheet of paper and fold it over 4 times. Use a ruler to estimate the thickness of this bundle, which now has 16 layers (see diagram above). Divide your measure by 16 to get the value for T – the thickness of one sheet. Suppose the folded bundle measured 1.6mm. A single sheet would then be 0.1mm thick, but remember to divide this by 1,000,000 to turn millimetres into kilometres (or turn the distance to the Moon into millimetres).

Compare your program with the one printed below. The answer is surprising, only 42 folds are needed to reach the Moon.

```
10 REM MOONTH
20 LET K=0
30 T=.0000001
40 REPEAT
50 LET T=T*2
60 LET K=K+1
70 UNTIL T>384400
80 PRINT K
90 END
```

73

Computer Languages

1. Machine language is the language of binary numbers that all computers actually work in. All programs have to be turned into machine language at some stage.

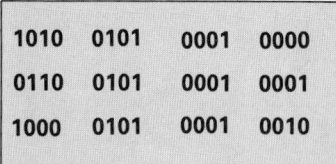

2. Assembly language is easier for humans to follow. These lines say: LoaD what is in box 10, ADd box 11 and STore the sum in box 12.

3. Programming languages are closer to human languages. One line of BASIC says the same as all the machine language above.

At first, programmers had to write all their programs in machine language. It took ages and mistakes (**bugs**) were hard to trace. So they invented **interpreter** programs, which make the computer translate other languages into machine language.

Nowadays, most programs are written in 'high-level' programming languages because they are so much easier to write and correct. But programs to control input, output and graphics are often written in assembly language because the computer can obey this more quickly.

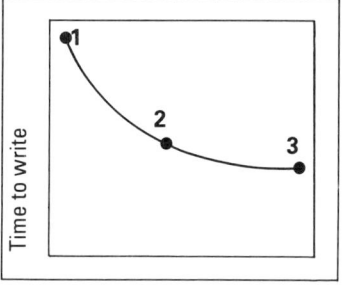

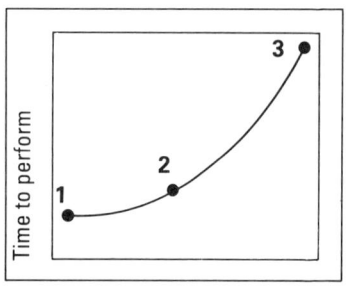

Programming languages

There are hundreds of different programming languages, each suited to different tasks. Large computers can be programmed in a number of them, whereas microcomputers can usually deal with only one – often BASIC. But there are also many different dialects of BASIC, so some changes are often needed to transfer a BASIC program from one computer to another (see page 43).

Although BASIC is one of the easiest languages to learn, it is not always the best to use. Long programs with lots of GOTO jumps can be difficult to follow. Other languages like ALGOL are better for complicated programs. LOGO, shown on the right, is easy for young children to learn.

FORTRAN is the oldest programming language, and can be used on most large computers. It is good for FORmula TRANslation and scientific jobs. COBOL is often used for business programs like handling accounts and mailing lists. A new, advanced language, called ADA after Ada Augusta (page 68), may become the universal language of the future.

LOGO

LOGO is a programming language which can be used to build up pictures from simple shapes. To make a flower, the first command is QCIRCLE, which draws a quarter circle.

Another QCIRCLE drawn at 90° to the first closes the shape to make a petal:
TO PETAL
QCIRCLE 50
RIGHT 90
QCIRCLE 50
RIGHT 90
END

To form a flower, the petal is REPEATed 4 times, each at 90° to the first
TO FLOWER
REPEAT 4
PETAL
RIGHT 90
END

Add more REPEATs, and a smaller turning angle:
TO FLOWER2
REPEAT 10
PETAL
RIGHT 36
END

Binary Code

As described on page 29, there are only two binary digits: 1 and 0. Your fingers can help you to work out binary numbers. Write the numbers 1,2,4,8 and 16 on the fingers of one hand, as shown on the right. Any number up to 31 can be built up by adding some of your finger numbers together. Pick a number and work out which fingers you need. Then write down the binary number 1 for each finger held up, and 0 for each finger held down (see examples opposite).

Now look at the table below. Can you see the pattern building up? Try writing down the next few numbers in the table.

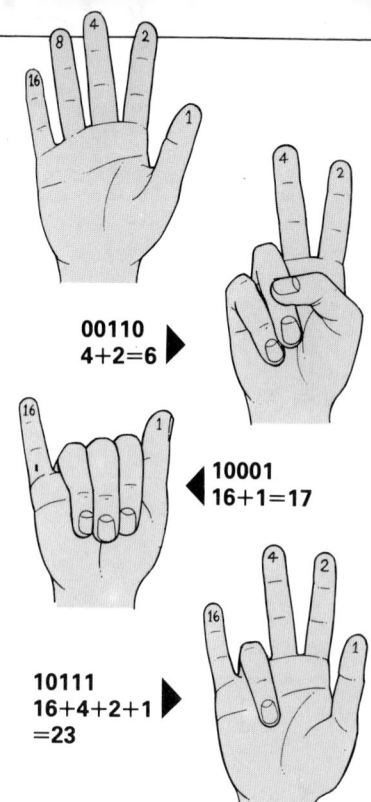

00110
4+2=6

10001
16+1=17

10111
16+4+2+1
=23

BASE-TEN	BINARY
1	00001
2	00010
3	00011
4	00100
5	00101
6	00110
7	00111
8	01000
9	01001

Bits and bytes

Each BInary digiT is called a **bit**. Most microcomputers process information in 8-bit chunks called bytes. A **byte** can store any number up to 256. It can also hold the code for any letter or symbol on the computer's keyboard. A thousand bytes make a **Kilobyte** or **K**. When you see advertisements for micros 'with 32 K of RAM', it means that their internal memory can hold about 32,000 letters and symbols (around 5000 words).

Although binary numbers look off-putting at first, doing addition in them is very easy, because there are really only four sums:

$$\begin{array}{r} 01 \\ +01 \\ \hline 10 \end{array}$$

$$\begin{array}{r} 01 \\ +10 \\ \hline 11 \end{array}$$

$$\begin{array}{r} 11 \\ +10 \\ \hline 101 \end{array}$$

$$\begin{array}{r} 11 \\ +11 \\ \hline 110 \end{array}$$

Longer sums are done by applying the same rules:

BASE-TEN	BINARY

$$\begin{array}{r} 6 \\ +17 \\ \hline 23 \end{array} \qquad \begin{array}{r} 00110 \\ +10001 \\ \hline 10111 \end{array}$$

Try working out the answers to these puzzles:

1. The binary code on page 74 can be seen as 12 groups of 4-bit numbers. Write down the base-ten value of each 4-bit number.

2. Write down the binary equivalents of 11 and 18. Try adding them in their binary form. Check your answer as $11+18=?$

3. What is the base-ten value of 111111?

4. $1000000-1=111111$. Convert this binary sum into base-ten numbers.

Answers

1. 10, 5, 1, 0; 6, 5, 1, 1; 8, 5, 1, 2; Rearranging these in pairs gives 105, 10; 65, 11; 85, 12. Now look again at the assembly language on page 74! 105 stands for LDA; can you guess what 65 and 85 are?

2. $1011+10010=11101$

3. $1+2+4+8+16+32=63$

4. $64-1=63$

77

Micros: Large and Small

These microcomputers are just a few of the hundreds on sale. Unless otherwise stated, screens and printers are bought separately. (Drawings not to scale.)

A rough price guide:
A=under £100
B=£100 to £299
C=£300 to £699
D=£700 to £1400
E=over £1400

Acorn/BBC

Its advanced design makes this BBC Micro very flexible. It is used in schools, and also in homes and by small businesses. BBC BASIC is built-in, but other languages can be used. Sound effects include musical chords. Screen display can show various letter sizes and graphics in 8 colours.

Model A: 16K RAM, price bracket B, can be expanded. Model B: 32K RAM, price bracket C. Can be used with teletext, Prestel, disc drives, and network.

Apple II

Apple II was one of the first best-selling personal computers, especially in USA. It has sound effects and colour graphics. Lots of software packages are available for schools and businesses, mainly in BASIC. However, Apple have now announced new models which may not be able to run the Apple II software.

Apple II: 16K or 48K RAM, price bracket C. Can be used with disc drives, graphics tablet, games paddles for use with computer games, a voice recognition unit and Prestel.

Commodore

PETs were the first mass-produced personal computers. Black-and-white screens are built-in, and disc drives can be added. PETs have limited graphics, and the design is now out-of-date. They are still widely used, however.

Other Commodore models are more up-to-date, but do not have built-in screens. The VIC 20 is popular for home use. The Commodore 64 has advanced graphics, a larger memory and can link with networks and Prestel.

PETs: 16 or 32 K RAM, price brackets C and D.
VIC 20: 16-colour graphics, sound and 5 K RAM, price bracket B.
Commodore 64: sound, advanced colour graphics and 64 K RAM, price bracket C.

Epson

The HX20 is the first personal computer from a company well-known for making printers. It is the size and weight of a large book, yet it has a full typewriter-style keyboard, a tiny screen and a printer. It also has a clock, calendar and alarm. It runs on rechargeable batteries and an adaptor to plug it into the mains is also available. Its RAM 'remembers' even when the computer is switched off. It is aimed at people in business and travellers.

HX20: 16 K RAM, price bracket C. Can be used with an extra 16 K RAM and a built-in miniature cassette recorder, both price bracket A. Connections to full-size printer and screen also available.

Osborne 1

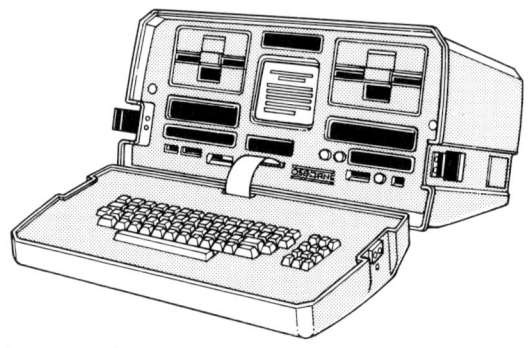

Described as 'a complete portable computer system', Osborne 1 is the size and weight of a small, heavy suitcase. It has a small screen, twin disc drives, and a full keyboard in its lid.

Osborne 1: 64 K RAM, price bracket D includes selected business software. It can be connected to a full-size screen, printer, telephone, battery pack, and extra disc drives.

Research Machines Ltd.

The 380Z was the first micro designed specially for schools and colleges. A lot of educational software exists for it. It can have disc drives built into it, or be used with a cassette player.

380Z: 32 or 64 K RAM, price brackets C or D. It can be used in a network.

The newer 480Z ranges from 32 to 256 K of RAM, price brackets C and D, with high resolution colour graphics an optional extra.

It can be linked in a network and is intended for use by young children.

Sharp

The PC 1500 is the size and weight of a standard pocket calculator, and its keyboard looks and feels similar. However, it is a true computer, programmable in BASIC, with serious uses in business and engineering. Programs are stored on cassette tapes. The built-in screen displays one line.

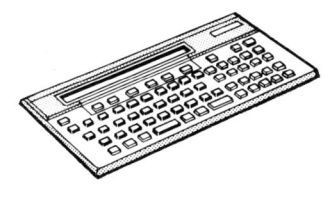

PC 1500: 3.5 K RAM, price bracket B. Can be used with extra RAM, batteries or a mains adaptor, and a colour printer (also price bracket B).

Sinclair

Sinclair's unique style of entering programs can help to prevent beginners' mistakes, once they have mastered the keyboard which has several symbols on each key. Sinclair machines connect with standard TVs and cassette recorders, but the printer needs special paper.

The ZX81 has 1 K RAM. Its low price (bracket A) quickly made it the world's fastest seller. Some people find its flat keyboard hard to use.

The Spectrum has moving rubber keys, colour, sound and 16 or 48 K RAM, price bracket B. Special 'Microdrives' to store software were to be available in 1983.

ZX81

Spectrum

Microdrive

Word Processing

If you use a typewriter to write a letter to a friend, you have to choose your words, find the letters on the keyboard and arrange the lines on the page all at the same time. Although you can correct small errors, any big mistakes mean that you will have to start again. If you're not used to the keyboard, it can take ages to get everything right.

Word processing is different in that each stage is separate. You start by typing in the words, which appear on the screen. Then you can **edit** (correct and rearrange) them as much as you like. Once you are satisfied that the content is right, you arrange the format (margins, spacing etc.). Finally you print out the finished letter.

The first word processors were specially built for that purpose and could do nothing else. They were also very expensive and sold mainly to large organisations that produced a lot of typewritten material. Now, any computer can process words if it has the right software.

The text for *Computer World* was written on a BBC Micro fitted with a word processing program on a chip.

The effect on offices

Word processing threatens the future of the copy typist's job. Word processor operators can produce perfect results faster. They need more skill than a copy typist, and are better paid. However, most secretaries do lots of other things besides typing; the day-to-day running of many offices depends on efficient and responsible secretaries. The art of dealing with a difficult customer, for example, would be extremely hard to computerize!

QWERTY rules?

All typewriters have a 'QWERTY' keyboard and so far nearly all computer keyboards have copied this arrangement of letters (see page 30). This is because it is the pattern that most people know. It dates back to the first, mechanical typewriters, which were so slow that often-used keys had to be kept apart. Otherwise a fast typist would have jammed the keys.

Thus, QWERTY is actually designed to slow the typist down! The experimental Maltron keyboard, shown below, is faster and easier to learn. It groups the letters more logically and its shape fits the human hand.

Experimental Maltron keyboard

Computer Puzzles

Each of these puzzles has computer words hidden in it. The words can be found by joining up the letters, using horizontal or vertical lines as shown in the example opposite. The lines can go in any direction and do not have to be straight. Some letters may be used in more than one word.

To help you find the words, there are clues for each puzzle. (The number given after each clue tells you how many letters make up the answer.)

The example on the right shows the words RAM, BYTE and DATA. The clue for RAM might have been 'Could be named after a male sheep (3)'.

EXAMPLE

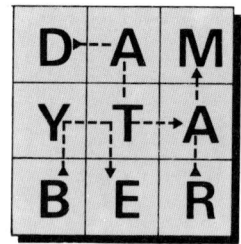

If you get stuck, remember that the Glossary on pages 88-91 may help. Also, the clues in each puzzle have been arranged in alphabetical order of the answers. So the first answer in a puzzle may begin with a B, and the last one with a letter near the end of the alphabet. The answers are given on page 91.

PUZZLE No. **1**

S	N	E	T	O
C	R	E	T	W
U	T	P	N	I
O	B	U	G	R
L	E	T	E	P

An insect's mistake (3).
Information put into the computer (5).
A BASIC instruction giving permission (3).
What input becomes (6).
A tame microcomputer (3).
Gives output on paper (7).
Displays information (6).
Equals binary 1010 (3).
Equals binary 10 (3).

PUZZLE No. 2

What computers work in (6).
Eight bits make one of these (4).
One of these is hard to eat (4).
A type of code shops use (3).
Memory which forgets when you switch off (3).
Memory which can only be 'read' (3).
What chips are made of (7).

E	S	I	P	R
T	I	L	I	A
Y	C	O	H	B
B	I	N	C	R
Y	R	A	M	O

PUZZLE No. 3

K	C	I	D	G
B	A	S	C	O
T	E	L	E	T
E	X	T	S	O
R	A	W	T	F

A common programming language (5).
A floppy one stores a lot of information (4).
This instruction would make you jump (4).
The size of a memory is given in this unit (1).
Software sent from afar (12).
Information transmitted with a television signal (8).

PUZZLE No. 4

Binary digits (4).
To correct or rearrange before you print (4).
This is where programs and data are stored (6).
You need a lot of these for good graphics (6).
This tells the computer what to do (7).
Basically short for a remark (3).

X	E	L	S	B
I	D	I	T	I
P	G	O	R	R
Y	R	A	P	E
R	O	M	E	M

Computer Careers

If you have found this book interesting, you might like to consider a job working with computers. There are various kinds of jobs. Here are a few examples.

Operating jobs
If you can type, you may want to do data preparation or control. This involves preparing information for the computer, and could lead on to a job operating it. Computer operators have to be reliable and careful.

Programming
To program a computer, you need to be systematic and willing to work at details. You don't *have* to be good at maths or have a university degree. Keenness and a logical approach are more important.

Systems analysis
This is a grand-sounding name for knowing whether and how to use a computer to solve a problem. Systems analysts may be promoted from senior programmers, or they may train for this job from the start. Most analysts are highly intelligent, but skill at communicating with people is just as important.

MORE BOOKS ABOUT COMPUTERS

Computers in Your Life by Melvin Berger (Thomas Crowell, 1981). Lively, illustrated descriptions of computers in action in the USA.

Using Computers by Lionel Carter and Eva Huzan (Knight Books, 1982). An introduction to programming in BASIC.

Working with Computers 3rd edition (1982), published by the National Computing Centre Ltd. Explains the various careers.

The Personal Computer Book by Robin Bradbeer, 2nd edition (Gower, 1982). Useful if you want to buy a computer.

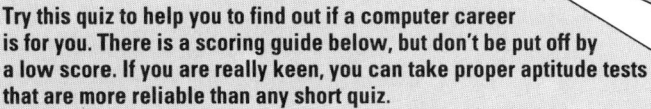

CAREER QUIZ

Try this quiz to help you to find out if a computer career is for you. There is a scoring guide below, but don't be put off by a low score. If you are really keen, you can take proper aptitude tests that are more reliable than any short quiz.

1. Do you tend to stop doing things part way through?
   a) only if interrupted b) sometimes c) often
2. Can you tell if a word is spelt correctly just by seeing if it 'looks right'?
   a) no b) sometimes c) often or always
3. Are you known to your friends and teachers as someone who keeps on working at a problem until you have solved it?
   a) definitely b) probably c) no
4. Do you spend much time on hobbies that need careful attention to detail, like needlework or stamp-collecting?
   a) no b) a little c) a lot
5. Did you try to work out the programming problem on page 73?
   a) no b) yes, but did not finish c) yes
6. Do you think that a job working with computers would be
   a) always interesting b) occasionally boring c) mostly boring
7. How did you come to read this book?
   a) bought or borrowed it from a library yourself b) was given or lent it c) was told to read it by a teacher or parent
8. Do you like to find out how things work?
   a) usually b) sometimes c) hardly ever
9. Do you pride yourself on thinking logically about problems?
   a) no b) to some extent c) yes
10. If you read a newspaper article where the same word is used a lot, would you notice if it sometimes had a capital letter and sometimes didn't?
    a) probably b) perhaps c) no

SCORING KEY

For questions 1, 3, 7, 8, 10, score a=2, b=1, c=0.
For questions 2, 4, 5, 9, score a=0, b=1, c=2.
For question 6, score a=1, b=2, c=0.
Under 6: It doesn't sound as if computers are for you.
6 to 12: It could be worth finding out more about jobs with computers.
13 plus: You should certainly consider a computing career.

87

Glossary

Analogue Something that varies continuously; the opposite of digital.

Artificial Intelligence Computer programs can 'learn' from experience and make a computer appear to behave with intelligence.

Assembly language A coded language which is easier for the computer to deal with than programming languages like BASIC.

Bar code A printed pattern of vertical bars of different widths, used by shops to code information about their goods.

BASIC The most popular programming language for microcomputers at present. (See also Dialect.)

Binary A system of counting that uses only two numbers (0 and 1), instead of the usual ten (0 to 9). Deep down, all digital computers work in binary.

Bit A binary digit (0 or 1).

Bug A mistake in a computer program.

Byte The 'chunk' of memory which a computer uses to store one letter or number. Eight bits make a byte. (See also Kilobyte.)

Chip A piece of silicon containing an electrical circuit.

Computer A machine that processes information electronically. Modern computers can be as small as a book or as large as a room.

Data Information (other than programs) which is put in the form of letters or numbers and fed into a computer for it to process.

Debug To remove mistakes, or bugs, from a program.

Decoder A device that turns data coded in one form into another form to make it suitable for the computer.

Dedicated Able to do only one job, usually because of a built-in program.

Dialect A particular version of a programming language. BASIC has hundreds of different dialects.

Digital Something that is separated into units; the opposite of analogue.

Disc A flat, circular sheet of magnetic material that can be used to store information. A **disc drive** is the special device which reads from and writes onto the disc. It is more expensive than a cassette recorder, but loading software from discs is much faster.

Display To produce letters and pictures from a computer onto a screen. Television sets and special monitors are both used for this.

Edit To rearrange or improve text or programs on a computer.

Flow chart A diagram that shows the main stages involved in solving a problem. Flow charts are especially useful to show how different choices can lead to different actions.

Graphics Pictures – as opposed to letters – which the computer can draw. The higher the quality, or resolution, of the pictures, the more memory the computer needs.

Hardware The actual equipment which makes up the computer and its input and output devices.

Input Anything you put into the computer. All input has to be turned into binary numbers before the processor can deal with it.

Integrated circuit A complicated electrical circuit printed onto a single chip. This invention was the basis of third and fourth generation computers.

Interpreter A program written in machine language that translates programs written in higher-level languages into machine language.

Kilobyte (K for short) is 1024 bytes. The size of a computer's memory is often described as so many K. 1K would store about half the words on this page.

Load To transfer a program from cassette or disc into the computer's internal memory. (See also Memory.)

Loop A bit of a program that is obeyed over and over again.

Machine language The language of binary 1s and 0s that the computer actually works in.

Mainframe A large, powerful computer that has a great many users who may be spread over a wide area, and who may use different programming languages.

Memory Software must be loaded into a computer's internal memory before it can process it. (See also RAM, ROM and Kilobyte.) Computers also have external memory (discs and cassettes), where software is stored long-term.

Microcomputer (or Micro) A small computer, often used by just one person or for only one purpose. Microcomputers are made with microprocessors. They tend to be much cheaper and smaller than earlier computers of similar power.

Microelectronics The use of electronic devices in which

lots of parts are combined (or integrated) in tiny circuits, usually on silicon chips.

Microprocessor A computer processor on a single tiny silicon chip.

Monitor A high-quality screen designed to display computer output. Monitors give better results than television sets but tend to cost more.

Network A system for linking one or more computers and terminals so that they can communicate with each other and share facilities like external memory.

Output Any result which comes from the computer is output. Usually output is in the form of text or graphics displayed on a screen or printed on paper.

Pixel 'Picture cells'. The tiny squares of light that make up pictures, or graphics, on the screen. (See also Resolution).

Prestel The first service to make computer information available to the general public. A special decoder is needed, together with ordinary telephones and televisions.

Printer A device that produces printed output when connected to the computer.

Processor The part of the computer that actually does the sums and makes the decisions. Sometimes also called the **central processing unit** (cpu).

Program A list of instructions for the computer to obey, written in a special language (see next entry).

Programming language A special language which can be translated into the machine's own language for the processor to obey. There are hundreds of different programming languages. (See also program, interpreter and BASIC).

Random Access Memory (RAM) Memory inside the computer where software is stored temporarily for processing. The contents of RAM can be searched through very quickly, but it is 'forgotten' when the computer is switched off.

Read Only Memory (ROM) The part of the computer's memory which stores software permanently. It is used for programs that are needed frequently. Unlike RAM, the contents of ROM are 'remembered' even when the computer is switched off.

Resolution A measure of quality in computer graphics. **High resolution** graphics can look the same as television pictures, whereas in **low resolution** graphics you can easily see the square blobs, or pixels.

Screen Output device which shows what the computer is doing. Ordinary television sets can be used this way, but a special monitor gives better results.

Software Programs and data for the computer.

System A computer system is made up of all the hardware – computer, input devices, output devices, external memory – and the software which together allow a computer to do useful work.

Telesoftware Software which is sent straight into a computer's memory over a distance, using telephone lines or television broadcasting.

Terminal A device for communicating with a computer. Usually terminals have a keyboard and a screen or printer, sometimes both. Large mainframe computers can be linked to many terminals over a distance.

Transistor An electronic device which can switch electric currents on or off, or increase their power. Transistors replaced valves in radios and were the basis of the second generation of computers.

Videodisc A disc the size of a long-playing record which can store huge amounts of information, for example in the form of moving pictures and computer software. With a suitable linking device, computers can 'read' information directly from a videodisc.

Voice recognition The process of 'understanding' human speech or of identifying people by their voices. Computers can do both of these in a very limited way if they have suitable software and a device called a voice recognition unit.

Word processing A system for editing, storing and rearranging words and sentences, and their arrangement on a page. It can be done by any computer with suitable software, a screen and a printer.

Answers to puzzles
on pages 84–85

Puzzle 1: BUG, INPUT, LET, OUTPUT, PET, PRINTER, SCREEN, TEN, TWO
Puzzle 2: BINARY, BYTE, CHIP, BAR, RAM, ROM, SILICON
Puzzle 3: BASIC, DISC, GOTO, K, TELESOFTWARE, TELETEXT
Puzzle 4: BITS, EDIT, MEMORY, PIXELS, PROGRAM, REM

Index

93

Acknowledgements

Photographs: p2–3 Rediffusion Computers; p4, p27, p55, p57 IBM; p5 Fairchild UK Ltd; p24(1) Monsanto; p24(2&4) BBC/ITT; p24(3) National Semiconductor; p24(5,6,7,8) Plessey Semiconductors Ltd; p31 (top) Logica; p31 (bottom), p50, p59 Dept. of Industry; p38 Microelectronics Education Programme; p51 (top) National Westminster Bank; p51 (bottom) NCR; p53 Open University; p54 NASA; p56 Ian Carpenter/Cambridge Educational Computing Research and Technology Centre; p61 New Scotland Yard; p83 PCD.

Artwork: p36-37 Computer graphics by David R F Walker, Lloyd Jenkinson, David Bennetts/Loughborough University; p6-7 Lynne Willey/John Martin Artists Ltd; All other artwork by Eagle Artists, Ron Hayward, James Dugdale.
Cover illustration: Chris Forsey.